By D. Mann:

The Money Shot
In Me I Trust
The Intruders

The Intruders

D. Mann

**Deviant Ways Publications**
PO Box 94 – Montrose, MN 55363
www.DeviantWaysPublications.com

"The Intruders"

Copyright © 2018 D. Mann

The names, characters, places and events are of the author's imagination and used fictitiously and any resemblance to actual persons, living or dead, businesses, events or locales is entirely coincidental.

Edited by Frederick Crandall

Cover Design by Cherie Foxley

ISBN: 978-0-692-13706-2

# The Intruders

# CHAPTER 1

Evan Hunt knew which house he was going to burglarize and he was pretty certain that the owners wouldn't be home for another hour or so. All he needed was ten or fifteen minutes, sometimes less if they made it easy and had all of their jewelry ready to go in decorative jewelry boxes or sitting on top of dresser drawers.

The place was dark, no lights on the inside and not even a porch light on, the same as it was last Tuesday when he'd scoped it out. Evan crouched amidst the trees in the lot across the street from the half a million-dollar home. A new Lexus drove past him and he held his breath but they didn't see him in his black slacks, dark green turtleneck and black sports coat.

When the coast was clear he bolted across the street and didn't stop until he was beside the three-car garage. The Sacramento air was warm this May evening and the shirt beneath his jacket was already sticking to his chest. After the last burglary a few weeks ago he twisted his shirt and watched the sweat pour out in streams. He knew the jacket played a huge part in making him so hot but he figured it necessary to fit into the neighborhood if seen, as well as needing the pockets to store his loot.

Evan checked the door at the side of the garage but it was locked. The last burglary had been that easy, having simply entered through an unlocked garage door, but maybe word was out and people were being a little more cautious now. That's okay, he liked a challenge.

Evan heard another vehicle coming up the street and he ran to the back of the garage and rounded the corner before the vehicle passed. There was a half moon in the star filled sky and it painted everything shades of gray and blue in the backyard. The house sat on at least a half-acre lot with a line of trees at the edge of the grass.

The nearest neighbor's house was half a football field length away and yellow light glowed out windows onto their backyard, but from what Evan could tell there was no one outside. At the back of the house where Evan stood was a stone patio with a custom built fire pit and a large gas grill built into a stone countertop at one edge of the patio. Double French doors led from the patio into the house but they, too, were locked. Double doors were often easy to break apart or he could simply bust out one of the panes of glass and reach in and unlock the doors, but that was all a last resort. If possible, Evan liked to make entrance without actually breaking anything.

When Evan was a teenager he used to like to take cars for joyrides and every car he stole was always with keys. It was surprising how many people left their keys right in the ignition of their vehicle, whether in their garage or even sitting in the driveway. Never had he hotwired a car - he didn't know how - nor popped a lock on a steering column and started it with a screwdriver, which he'd read only works on older cars, which were harder to find in the neighborhoods he frequented.

This neighborhood, for instance, was a gated community with two guard shacks at either end of the development and a roving security truck that had already gone by the house twenty minutes ago and wouldn't be back around for another twenty minutes. It was a great place to commit burglaries because most homeowners put their security in the hands of the professionals and thought that meant they didn't need to do anything for themselves. Typical rich person mentality.

Evan walked around the house looking for any unlocked windows, and finding none, found himself trying the front door, which was also locked. He looked under the welcome mat that was shaped like a cloud and said 'Our Dream House.' There was no key there. He felt atop the ledge of the doorframe but only found dust. There were three porcelain cat statues at the side of the front door steps, all of them white. The second statue he looked under produced a house key. "Good kitty," Evan said with a smile as he used his coat sleeve to wipe the sweat from his brow.

The moment of truth, Evan thought as he stood at the front door and inserted the key into the lock. There were no alarm signs posted in the front yard, no stickers of warning on any of the windows or doors. But that was no guarantee that the place wouldn't be wired. Of course, even if all of those warnings had been present, Evan would still unlock the door and open it because at least two out of three times even people with alarm systems didn't actually utilize them.

Evan held his breath and could feel his heart beating in his throat as he turned the key and disengaged the deadbolt with a satisfying clunk. He turned the doorknob and pushed the door open a foot, his ears on high alert for any sort of buzzing sound that would come from an alarm keypad awaiting a disarm code. There was nothing...except the sound of a car coming down the street faster than most.

Evan stepped inside the dark house and slammed the door shut harder than he meant to. He peeked out a curtained side window at a small, red BMW that went racing past the front of the house.

Holy shit, what a rush, he thought as he turned to face the dark innards of the house. He tried to swallow but his mouth was dry and his whole body felt tingly and alive. No matter how many times he did this, each time was as exciting as the first as he realized anything could happen at any moment.

Time's a wastin', he thought and rushed in the direction that he figured was the master bedroom. He liked the fact that this was a single-story ranch style house because he was always afraid of getting trapped on second floors if somebody came home. He didn't think he'd be able to overcome his fear of heights and jump if it came down to it, so he tended to target one-story dwellings.

There was a set of double doors to the master bedroom, one of which was open. The bedroom was larger than Evan's living room and the king sized bed was empty as he expected, but one always had to make sure. Before getting started Evan went to the master bathroom and flipped up the toilet lid and seat. He unzipped his pants and pulled out his dick and let loose with a massive stream.

He didn't know what it was but every time he did a burglary he had to piss like a racehorse. He was sure it was nerves and he'd stopped trying to fight it after the first couple of times. So he learned to just go with the flow and it felt so damn good as the whiz coursed out his main vein. He tilted his head back as the sound of splashing water echoed off the bathroom tiles.

And then he caught the movement out of the corner of his eye. It was a shadowy figure moving slowly, almost seeming to be tiptoeing past the bathroom door in the master bedroom.

"Hey, uh," Evan said as he cut off the stream and shoved his dick in his pants. He wasn't sure how he was going to explain this, but then he didn't have to as the figure took off running.

Oh shit, Evan thought, wondering if the person was going first for a gun or a phone. He wasn't about to stick around and find out as he ran out of the bathroom. He ran out of the bedroom and down the hall but rather than turn toward the front door he went for the double French doors he knew led to the backyard. If the police or security were on the way he didn't want to be seen exiting out the way they'd be coming in.

One of the French doors was open which Evan was thankful for so he didn't have to waste time unlocking them. But as he rushed onto the stone patio he remembered the doors being locked when he'd checked them less than five minutes earlier. And then he saw the figure running along the back tree line away from the house.

Wait a fucking second, Evan thought, and began running after the figure. Obviously this wasn't the homeowner running away from their home because if it was they would have run toward the neighbor's lighted backyard, not the dark woods. Something primal in Evan's brain made him chase that which was running away. And like a dog chasing a car, he wasn't sure what he would do when he caught it, but he knew he had to go after it.

He was about forty yards behind as the figure dashed out of the woods and across a street. Evan followed, gaining ground as they ran along someone else's property line and across their backyard. They went down a small hill that flattened to an empty playground. A knee high fence made of thick, weathered logs partitioned the park from the gravel parking lot and the running figure tripped and did a great Superman impression landing head first in a cloud of dust. Evan leaped over the fence and stopped behind the dark clad figure laying face down.

"I didn't take anything," the figure said through gasps. "I didn't do anything."

"Don't move!" Evan said, not exactly sure why or what he was doing. What was he going to do, say he caught this person breaking into a place he was breaking into? What are the fucking odds, he thought - of all the houses this guy could be robbing and he's in the same one as Evan. There's probably a better chance of being struck by lightning or winning the lottery. But Evan was even more fascinated with the fact that this was the first criminal, other than himself, that he'd ever came across in his life.

"I'm sorry," the figure said and that's when Evan realized it wasn't a guy at all, it was a woman. She started to push herself up from the ground.

"I said don't move," Evan told her.

She lay back down on the ground. "I really didn't take anything. You can frisk me if you want."

Evan smiled and thought, why not. She was wearing black Spandex pants that hugged her slender legs like a tight glove. Evan bent over her and ran his hands from her knees up the side of her legs to her hips. He didn't know what the fuck he was doing; he'd never been frisked nor ever frisked anyone before, just what he'd seen in movies. But it was kind of fun. He slipped his hands over her ass which had a nice firm hump to it.

"Hey!" she said.
"Do you want to go to jail?"
"No."
"Do you have any weapons?"

"No."

She was wearing a black long sleeved shirt that fit her snuggly. The back had ridden up and was showing a couple inches of milky white skin above her yoga pants. That was enough flesh to get things hardening in Evan's pants as he slid his hands up the woman's sides, his fingers grazing the edges of her breasts before coming to her armpits.

A vehicle turned a corner heading toward the park. Evan froze, his hands on the woman's shoulders and then he crouched down next to her on one knee.

"What are you doing?" she asked. She rolled onto her side and looked at Evan. She had dark hair in a ponytail and a dark scarf tied around her forehead. Her breasts were stuffed into her tight shirt and were larger than Evan imagined. "Who are you?" she asked.

The truck slowed as it neared the parking lot. It had a light bar atop its roof. It was either a cop or security and Evan didn't feel like sticking around to find out which.

"Run!" Evan said to her. As he stood he grabbed her arm and pulled her to her feet.

The night lit up with blue and red flashing lights and a loud speaker blared: "Stop right there!"

Evan tugged the woman back the direction they came and they ran through the park. The woman jerked her arm out of Evan's grasp and they both ran as fast as they could.

The truck with the flashing lights had to drive in the opposite direction to get around the log fence and enter the park. "I command you to stop!" the loud speaker blared.

"No, this way!" Evan said to the woman who had started to go up the hill at the edge of the park. She hesitated a moment and then followed Evan as he raced across a soccer field. The truck's engine could be heard revving and getting closer. On the other side of the soccer field the grass sloped down and they pushed through some waist high bushes and dropped two feet into a dried up culvert.

"Come on," Evan said, breathing hard, his golden hair plastered to his sweaty head.

"Where's this go?" the woman asked.

"I know," Evan replied as he ran as fast as his burning legs and lungs would allow.

The truck had stopped some distance behind them and couldn't be seen except for the sporadic flashes of red and blue light reflecting off of bushes.

Evan climbed up the other side of the culvert and turned to help the woman but she was already beside him, and they made it to the top of the hill. They stood in front of a six-foot tall iron picket fence with ornamental spikes at the top.

"Where to now?" the woman asked, trying to catch her breath.

"Over."

She shook her head. "I don't think I can."

Sirens could be heard in the distance getting closer.

"Yes you can," Evan said. "I'll help you." He positioned himself next to the fence. "Step on my thigh here, then up onto my shoulders and over."

"Hold on, let me catch my breath." She put her hands on her knees as she took deep breaths.

"We've got to hurry," Evan told her as he kept looking around.

"That wasn't your home, was it?" she asked.

Evan couldn't help smiling as he shook his head.

"You jerk," she said and slapped his chest. "What were you doing feeling me up?"

"You said I could if I wanted to."

"You owe me a set of lock picks."

"You can pick locks?" Evan asked in amazement. "Can you teach me?"

"No."

There was more than one set of sirens growing closer.

"Come on," Evan said, bracing himself next to the fence. "We've got to go now."

She grabbed the fence with one hand while putting the other on Evan's shoulder and then she stepped up onto his thigh. Her breasts rubbed against his chest and face and then she was climbing atop his shoulders. She braced a foot between the ornamental spikes.

"Just jump over," he told her.

"I know what I'm--aaah!" Her foot slipped off the fence and she began to fall. Evan thrust his hands upward, one catching her ass and the other cupping her like a unicycle seat. He felt her heat as he held her aloft until she got her footing again on his shoulder.

"There!" a voice yelled from somewhere behind them in the culvert.

The woman pushed off from Evan, her foot kicking the side of his face as she vaulted over the fence and landed hard on the other side.

Evan took a few steps backwards as the security guard climbed out of the culvert and reached for him. Evan ran and jumped onto the fence, pulling himself up and flying himself over, his years as a gymnast letting him land smoothly on the other side.

"Come back here!" the security guard yelled at the two of them as they disappeared in a line of trees.

After a couple minutes of running Evan noticed the woman was limping. "Are you okay?" he asked.

"Let's just get out of here," she replied and kept running.

They came to the back of a strip mall and Evan could see a tear in the thigh of her Spandex pants. Blood was dripping onto the ground beneath her.

"Give me your scarf," Evan said, pulling it from her head before she replied. He began to wrap it around her wounded thigh.

"Trying to feel me up again, you perv?"

He tightened the scarf and she winced. "Sorry," he said.

"I've got to go," she said. In the light of the street lamps Evan realized she was a lot younger than he thought.

"My place is close by," Evan said.

"No, I've had enough of you, Chester Molester."

"Where's your car?"

"None of your business."

"You don't look so good. You should sit down."

"I'm fine," she said and then her eyes rolled back in her head and she fell.

# CHAPTER 2

"I'm not falling for that," the man built like a bulldog said. His complexion looked dark at first glance but only because of the dark hair on his arms and the week old growth on his face. His nose looked wider than it was only because it had been busted four times, three of those in the ring. He was sitting in the driver's seat of a grey Dodge Charger that everyone in the hood knew was an unmarked.

"What, you think I'm going to rip you off?" the tall Nigerian woman in the passenger seat asked. She was bone thin, pretty face, tiny tits in a padded black bra beneath a black mesh half top. A pair of dark purple shorts barely stayed on her curveless body when she walked.

"You're not that stupid," the cop told her.

"You've got that right. So give me the money."

"Go get the shit and then you get the money."

"But how am I supposed to get it without the money?"

"Figure it out. I'll be back in fifteen."

"Fox, don't do me like this," she pleaded.

"Out."

Nanae got out of the car and Detective Bryce Fox took off out of the alley without a second glance.

It took her less than ten minutes to suck the dopeman's dick and be standing in the shadows when the Charger rolled back into the alley. The car stopped barely long enough for her to get in and then was rolling out of the alley and out of the hood.

Ten minutes later they were in a motel room at the Regent Inn south of downtown. The Sacramento Sheriff's Department was always running stings out of these rooms so it was nothing for Fox to get one free of cost any time he wanted.

Though Nanae was wearing flats she was still a couple inches taller than Fox's five-seven. She stood with her body rubbing against his beefy arm, looking at him like an expectant puppy awaiting a treat.

"Go clean up," he said to her.

"I already showered," Nanae replied. "I ain't done no tricks tonight."

"Oh, you just got this for free?" Fox said holding up a two inch square clear baggie filled with yellowish chunky powder.

"I only sucked his--"

"I don't want to hear what the fuck you did."

"You asked."

"I was being facetious. Now wash up," he said and motioned with his hand, the little meth baggie swinging from his fingers.

"Can't I just get a little--"?

"No. Go. I'm getting mad."

Nanae looked at the baggie over her shoulder as she ran the three steps to the bathroom.

When she came out of the bathroom five minutes later she was wearing a green towel wrapped around her beanpole body, tucked under her armpits and reaching to mid thigh. Her skin was still wet and glistened like a city street after a rain. Fox was sitting on the double bed, his back to her, and on the nightstand next to him was a small glass pipe with a bulbous end balanced over a white Bic lighter. Nanae's heart began to race and her body tingled at the thought.

"Can I?" she asked as she stepped in front of Fox.

He looked up at her and smiled and nodded his head. She snatched the warm pipe and lighter from the nightstand, stuck the stem eagerly into her mouth and set flame to the bottom of the bubble. The crusty substance inside the bubble began to turn into white smoke, a small stream escaping from the tiny hole in the top of the bubble. Nanae sucked the smoke through the stem and inhaled deeply.

"You charred the pipe," Fox said.

Nanae shook her head.

"Yeah you fucking did, look at it."

There was a film of black soot on the bottom of the glass bubble.

"Why have you been so aggravating tonight?"

Nanae exhaled a large cloud of gray smoke and she almost felt like she would float with it to the ceiling. It wasn't the best meth she had, there was an aftertaste in her mouth like gas and plastic, but it still did the trick.

"Sorry," she said and offered him the pipe and lighter.

He shook his head.

"You might be," he told her. "Bend over my lap."

Nanae lay across Fox's lap in her green towel.

"You've been bad on purpose, haven't you?" he said.

"Yes," she replied.

Fox pulled the edge of the towel up over her flat ass. As he did so, Nanae hit the pipe again, heating it up and sucking in the smoke.

The cop's heavy hand came down on her ass cheek with a loud slap and she grunted but held the smoke in. His hand smacked her ass again, sending warm tingles throughout her body. She exhaled the smoke and her thighs quivered. Fox spanked her again and this time she cried out, as she knew he wanted to hear.

"Set that shit down before you burn yourself," he said. She stretched out each hand and placed the lighter and pipe on the nightstand.

"Are you going to stop being a pain," he said and smacked his hand on her rump causing her to squeal, "in my ass?"

"I'll do anything you say," she told him. She could feel the bulge in his jeans pressing against her side.

He spanked her again and this time left his hand on her tender flesh, making small circular motions.

"Spread your legs," he said and she did. His hand slipped between them and felt the warmth and moisture of her smooth pussy. He rubbed his hand back and forth and Nanae moaned and wiggled her ass against his hand.

"Get on the bed," he demanded.

Nanae stood and removed her towel as Fox watched. Her breasts were the size of chocolate cupcakes topped with black peanut M&M's. He couldn't remember her age, twenty-something, and she had some barely visible stretch marks from at least one child. The only color other than black was the white of her eyes and the faint pink of her extruding labia.

She laid the towel atop the ugly brown and gold bedspread and then lay atop it on her back. Fox stood and undid his pants, pulling a three pack of condoms from his back pocket before letting the jeans fall to the floor.

"Hun-unh, roll over," he told her.

Nanae rolled over onto her belly, repositioning her body so it was lying atop the towel. Fox removed his shirt and dropped it atop his jeans. He tore open one of the condom packages, tossing the other two on the nightstand, and slipped it over his protruding cock.

Nanae grabbed a pillow from the head of the bed and pushed it underneath her hips as Fox got onto the bed behind her. His hands grabbed her toothpick legs and he spread them further apart as he guided the tip of his cock toward its pink target.

"Uuhhh," Nanae moaned as his manhood sank into her.

Fox's pelvis pressed against Nanae's ass cheeks and then he began thrusting back and forth. His right hand slapped her right ass cheek and then a few thrusts later his left hand slapped her left ass cheek.

"You like that, don't you," he grunted.

"Oh yeah, you know it," she replied as she did to all her tricks. Not that she wasn't enjoying herself, but what she really came for was on the nightstand.

"Oh yeah," Fox grunted and he gripped her bony hips as he rammed his cock back and forth harder and faster into her slippery hole.

"Oh yeah," she cried out, "fuck me!"

"Oh yeah," he grunted. "Oh yeah, Oh yeah!"

She thought he sounded like the Kool-Aid man and bit her lip to keep from laughing. The last thing in the world she wanted to do was piss off Fox and laughing at a man while he's fucking you was a good way to get yourself hurt in this business.

Nanae cried out a few oh gods at what she thought was the right time and she was duly rewarded with the pipe after they were both leaning against pillows at the head of the bed.

"You gonna give me that money?" Nanae asked after they were back in his car and driving into the city.

"You're kidding, right?" Fox said. "Why would I do that?"

"You know why. The dope."

"The dope that you smoked?"

"Not all."

"You seriously gonna bust my balls on this?"

"You know I don't charge you for bustin' your nut."

Fox laughed. "Damn right you don't. As good as I give it to you, I'm the one that should be charging."

Isn't that what every man thought. She decided to try a different tactic though she was pretty certain it was a hopeless cause.

"I lost money," Nanae told him. "I coulda been workin' tonight. But I spent it with you."

He looked over at her and smirked. "All you'd do with the money is get high. I got you high and you had a good time."

"I do have a child to feed."

"I thought you lost that to social services?"

"My mama's got custody now."

"So your mama's got a child to feed?"

"I try to help out."

"I'll tell you what," Fox said as he neared her neighborhood, "you get me that info on Hilo and I'll see that you get more than a good time."

"Come on, Fox, can't I just get a little?"

He stopped the car at a dark corner. "Don't start whining on me," he told her. "Now get out."

"I'll try to get that," Nanae said as she slid out of the car seat.

"Don't fucking try. Do it." He punched the gas chirping the tires as he sped out of the hood.

It was a little after midnight when Fox walked into the backroom of Rusty's. Four guys all in their forties like Fox, were sitting around an eight person poker table, each with colored playing chips, two face down cards and one or more glasses of alcohol in front of him. All the men were in casual civilian clothes.

"Look what the cat dragged in," Detective Ken Hansel said. He had a horse face with cropped wheat colored hair.

"Fuckin' Fox, oh great," Sergeant Jack Mellanski said. His gray wavy hair and his rank made most people think he was the oldest of the bunch but he was actually the youngest having just turned forty-one.

"You better have brought some money," Detective Clive Winters said. "Your credit is no good." Winters reminded Fox of a dirty snowball with his black and gray short hair and portly figure.

Detective Leonard Cole kept his cold eyes on the table and said nothing. He was the oldest at forty-eight with a bald head and well groomed dark mustache and beard that rose into sideburns to the tops of his ears.

"Fuck you, Winters," Fox said. "If I remember correctly, you owe me a couple hundred."

"I don't owe you shit. You lost that at horseshoes."

"Matter of fact," Hansel said, "you still owe me from horseshoes. You can't toss to save your life."

"Oh shit, here we go," Fox said as he sat at one of the chairs around the poker table.

"Where you been all night?" Sergeant asked.

Fox set a few hundred dollars on the green felt table. "Taking care of business."

"Since when is there any business more important than this room?" Hansel asked.

"Can we finish this hand?" Cole asked the table. "You can all jerk each other off afterward."

"Well we know who's holding the pocket pair, don't we?" Sergeant said.

Fox looked at Cole who avoided his gaze. "Naw, he ain't got but a king and a queen, maybe a jack."

"Fuck you, Fox," Cole said, looking at him for the first time.

Fox smiled. "Yep, definitely the jack."

"I'm all in," Winters said pushing his stack of chips into the middle.

"Fuck all y'all," Cole said throwing in his cards and standing up from the table. He was a half-foot taller than Fox, lean and wiry.

The other four men laughed.

"Cash me out," Cole said and downed his highball glass.

"What, you're quitting'?" Winters asked.

"I don't play with people whose math is different than mine," Cole said looking at Fox.

The laughter stopped as Fox stood up. "I already told you--"

"Hey!" Sergeant said as he glanced to make sure the door to the private card room was still closed. "I already told you both it's squashed. I don't want to hear no more about it."

"I didn't bring it up," Fox said.

"Of course you didn't," Cole said, "'cause you're not the one out almost ten grand. No, instead you somehow end up with an extra twenty grand."

"Bullshit!" Fox said. "The day you take some stripper whore's word over your partners' is the day you might as well turn in your badge."

"Godammit! I said knock it off!" Sergeant yelled as he stood up, his gut jostling the poker table and knocking over stacks of chips. "If I hear another fucking word about this I'm going to beat both your asses to a pulp. It's done. I don't know how it got fucked up or how that little job went south, but it let us see that we're getting sloppy and we need to tighten things up otherwise it will be our asses. If that happens there won't be enough money in the world to save us. So I mean it, drop it for good because if either of you mention that money again I'm putting someone in a hole."

"Does that mean I don't get my horseshoe winnings?" Hansel asked.

"Looking at that pile of chips in front of you," Fox said as he sat down, "it looks like you've got a horseshoe stuck up your ass."

Sergeant sat down and looked at Cole. "You playing?"

"Next time," Cole said. "I'm cashing in tonight." He pushed his chips toward Sergeant.

"Who do I gotta blow to get a drink around here?" Fox asked.

"Loretta was just in here," Hansel said.

"I'd blow her," Winters said.

"She's probably got a bigger dick than you do, Winters," Fox said and the guys laughed.

Fox watched Cole leave the backroom and he wondered not for the first time if he was going to have to take care of that problem before the problem tried to take care of him. He saw Sergeant looking at him and Fox nodded his head and smiled as if everything was all right. But everything was far from all right.

# CHAPTER 3

"Sir, is everything alright? Sir?" The doorman of the five star Le Rogue hotel asked. He bent down to the man sitting on the sidewalk whose back was against the brick exterior of the building. The man was wearing a three thousand dollar dark blue suit and Italian loafers and sat staring into the middle of the street. His eyes never blinked.

"Oh, no," the doorman said as he pulled his cell phone from his coat pocket. He stumbled forward to one knee and inadvertently put his hand on the dead man's chest to steady himself. The dark fabric of the man's suit was squishy and warm. The doorman jerked his hand back and his palm was painted in blood. With the thumb of his other hand he dialed 9-1-1.

Five miles away the killer reassembled his smart phone after removing it from the Faraday bag. Simply taking the battery out of the phone did not completely turn off the phone and with sophisticated enough equipment it could still be tracked. Only by placing the phone in a tightly woven copper mesh bag that was folded over itself to prohibit any chance of an incoming or outgoing signal assured some sense of security. And even then Marco wouldn't free his phone until he was at minimum five miles away from any finished job. Were he to be pulled over and arrested right now there was no electronic signals that could place him at Le Rogue nearly ten minutes ago.

Marco was driving a black turbo Porsche and the phone came to life in his lap. Marco brought up the last number he had called earlier in the evening and pressed the 'Call' button.

When it was answered on the second ring Marco said, "I'm coming to get you."

Marco pulled into the driveway of the upper middle class town home, one of three residences that he owned in the New Orleans area. His cell phone had been taken apart and put back into the Faraday bag while he was on the freeway fifteen minutes prior. There was nothing to link him to this home except for the person inside. The garage door opened and the Porsche entered and Marco waited for the garage door to close before exiting the vehicle.

He was dressed in a black Christian Dior suit with a black shirt and black silk tie. His feet were clad in soft-soled black leather shoes that he could move quickly and quietly in. After every assassination he would incinerate every article of clothing he wore on the job just in case the victim's blood or a stray hair might have gotten on him or a fiber of his clothing were left on the victim. But tonight was the first time he'd ever made an exception to the rule because he had a second obligation that he had to attend to.

He should know better, he thought as he entered the town home from the garage. Even though tonight's hit couldn't have gone any smoother and he was certain there had been no witnesses, no cameras, no errors, he should stick with his protocol that had thus far kept him alive and out of jail. He contemplated at least changing into another suit - he could hide this one in one of his hidden stash spots until taking it to the incinerator - but then he saw her, his kryptonite.

Ophelia was standing in the opulent living room wearing the stunning red and silver Chanel evening gown that he'd paid over two grand for earlier in the day and the Christian Louboutin three inch leather heels which had cost over half that. Add the five thousand dollars for the diamond pendant around her neck and matching earrings he'd gotten her last month and another three grand for the Prada clutch, and still it came nowhere near close to her actual worth.

"What?" she said in her Persian accent that drove Marco wild. Especially when she said his name, and she knew this. "Do I look okay, Marco?"

"You are more beautiful than a rainbow in the desert," he told her, a hint of his French accent-adding flavor to his words. He could speak without his accent but he knew she liked it.

Ophelia's red painted lips parted in a smile upon hearing his words. He was quoting from a book that he had been reading aloud to her as they sat together in the whirlpool tub last week. She loved how thoughtful and sensitive he was and for how attentive he was to her. "Oh, Marco," she said and parted her arms to him.

Marco took her into his arms and lifted her off her feet, her breasts pressing against his muscular chest. She kissed his eyebrow, his cheek, and his lips. Especially his lips and he pushed his tongue into her mouth. She tasted the tingly Mentos candy he had been sucking on before arriving at the town home. She could also feel him growing hard against her body and she liked how easily excited he got with her.

He set her down but continued to hold her close to him. His chocolate brown eyes melted in her sparkling blue eyes that were so perfect and rich he had accused her of wearing contacts when he'd first met her two months ago. In her heels she was only a couple inches shorter than his five-ten and she held his gaze.

"You always look at me like that," Ophelia said, a blush coming over her.

"Like what?"

"Like, I don't know. Like a kid about to open a present on Christmas morning."

"That's because I can't wait to unwrap you."

She smiled and kissed his clean-shaven chin. She liked his soft, smooth face and his dimpled chin. His skin was olive complexioned like hers, but where she'd been born in Iran his bloodline came from Spain. They both had black hair, his short and perfectly gelled in place while hers was long and straight and reaching almost to her waist.

"That sounds wonderful," she said. "Does that mean we are not going to the gala?"

"You look too beautiful not to take out. I'll unwrap you later."

Marco was a fabulous dancer, his control and handling of Ophelia making her feel like Cinderella at the ball. With a squeeze of his hand or a slight pull or push he'd signal his next move to her and she'd know to spin or dip or swoon. She felt like she was on a roller coaster custom built for the two of them and she could see the eyes of envy upon them from other dancers.

Ophelia didn't know how she'd gotten so lucky to meet Marco and some days she'd think it was only a matter of time until he dumped her. She saw the way other women looked at him and flirted with him, women half her age. Marco was only thirty-three and in four months she'd be forty, even though she took care of herself and was easily mistaken for thirty. Why wouldn't Marco want a young, firm and toned model in her twenties, or half a dozen different ones? It wasn't that Ophelia was insecure or the jealous type, but she was a realist and knew Marco could have whatever he wanted.

He told her he wanted her and he showered her with gifts, denied her nothing, and she wasn't quite sure why. She was less than a year out of a shitty nine-year marriage to a U.S. military man that shouldn't have lasted more than a year. Her ex-husband had been emotionally abusive and though he'd never gotten physical with her he'd punched, kicked, and thrown practically every possession they'd owned at one time or another. Ophelia had a temper and had punched, kicked and thrown as much back.

With Marco there was none of that; they had not had a single fight. There had been a few times in the beginning when she got a little frustrated when she couldn't reach him on his phone and it would go straight to voicemail as if it were off. But he explained that he didn't like communicating on phones, that they were only useful to him for setting up face to face meetings, and he would constantly lose or break his phone and be getting new ones. He'd had three different phone numbers since she'd known him.

"Thirsty?" he asked her as a song ended.

"Parched."

"Where were you?" he asked as he led her through the well-dressed crowd to the marble covered bar.

"I was just thinking," she said with a smile.

He ordered her an Appletini and a gin and tonic for himself. "You're always thinking. About what?"

"When you met me at the ship," she said.

"You two met on a ship?" a beautiful, busty blonde said standing next to them at the bar.

"Hello, Maggie," Marco said to the blonde in the black cocktail dress. "Ophelia, this is Maggie, Dmitri's wife. Maggie, this is Ophelia."

The two women shook hands.

"You looked magnificent on the dance floor," Maggie told Ophelia.

"I was just along for the ride," Ophelia said and the both of them laughed. Marco smiled and handed Ophelia her drink before taking a sip from his own.

"So tell me about this ship you two were on," Maggie said. "I love cruises. Marco never likes to talk about himself."

Ophelia took a sip of her drink and then said, "Oh, no, we weren't on a cruise together. I was taking a cruise with my mother and sister; we were leaving port in Miami. But before I got on the ship I met Marco at a pastry shop and he wanted to talk but I told him I had to go. He said he'd wait for me to come back but I told him he was crazy, that our cruise was seven days, but he assured me he would be waiting for me at the pastry shop. And he was."

"How romantic," Maggie said. She nodded her head at Marco and said, "He's one of a kind. He and my husband like to go to the track."

"The track?" Ophelia asked, looking at Marco and then back at Maggie.

"Oopsie," Maggie said and put her fingers to her mouth. "Does she not know about any of your vices?" she said to Marco.

Nor does anyone else, Marco thought. During the week in Miami while he awaited Ophelia's return, he'd killed a husband and wife on their yacht and made it look like a murder/suicide at sea. He normally left town immediately after a job but he had made an exception to his rule for this woman that he fell instantly and madly in love with. Kind of like him still wearing the same suit he'd killed a man in earlier this evening. It seemed he was breaking a lot of his rules lately.

"I don't think it's considered a vice as long as you're winning," Marco said and they all laughed. "I'm going to go to the restroom," he told Ophelia, "will you be alright?"

She loved how he was always checking to see if she was comfortable and happy. He was always putting her first which was something she'd never experienced in a relationship before. In her culture women were never put first, they were only there to serve their man.

"Of course she'll be alright," Maggie said, "she'll be here with me."

"Maybe that's what I'm worried about," Marco joked and gave the ladies a wink.

When he returned from the restroom he saw a man in his forties talking to the women. The man was six-two wearing a Brooks Brothers suit and a two hundred dollar haircut and he kept touching Ophelia and Maggie as he told some story he obviously thought was fetching.

"And so I said I'd grab it too if I were you!" the man said and put his hand on Ophelia's shoulder. His voice was deep like that of a movie trailer voice over. The women laughed and all three smiled as Marco approached.

Maggie made the introduction. "Marco, this is--"

"Hank Cruz," the man bellowed and thrust out his right hand, his left hand still on Ophelia.

Marco took the man's hand in his and squeezed. "Pleased to meet you," Marco said, though his eyes told the man that was a lie. Looking at Maggie, he asked, "Is he a friend of Dmitri's?"

"No, he just introduced himself to us."

Marco squeezed harder. The man's other hand left Ophelia's shoulder and clasped Marco's hand. "That's quite a grip," the man said, his voice a little higher. "I was just--"

"Leaving," Marco said.

The man nodded his head, his eyes glassy, his teeth gritted.

"Don't touch what isn't yours," Marco said, only loud enough for Hank's ears. He gave a final squeeze and tug on Hank's hand and the man stumbled away from the bar.

"Marco, are you okay?" Ophelia asked.

"Of course. Splendid. It's been a long day, I think I'm just getting tired."

Ophelia moved close to him and he could feel her breath on his ear as she said, "Not too tired I hope."

Ophelia had been in the bathroom for nearly twenty minutes. Marco was sitting atop his king sized bed in a pair of silk blue pinstripe boxers. The bedroom was lit by three large candles on one of the marble topped nightstands and soft instrumental music played from a Bose stereo atop the matching marble topped dresser.

The master bath door opened and Ophelia stood framed in the white light behind her. She looked like an angel in a white lace bra and panties and she wore a sheer mini robe that was fringed with white feathers.

"Good, you haven't fallen asleep yet," she said.

"That's where you're wrong," Marco replied, "because I have to be dreaming."

She smiled as she turned off the bathroom light and walked toward the bed. The flickering candlelight bounced off her body in a dance of shadows. She crawled onto the end of the bed and approached Marco like a white lioness, her eyes eating him up. He sat propped against the pillows watching her, his mouth open, his breathing getting heavy. She stopped inches in front of him on her hands and knees, the dark valley of her cleavage drawing him in.

She leaned forward, her long dark hair hanging down and brushing across his thighs and then his chest as she ran her tongue across his chin and along his jaw line and then to his ear. "I want you to be still," she whispered and then sucked on his ear lobe.

"Mmm," he moaned and brought his hand up to cup her breast.

She pulled his hand away and put it back on the bed. "That's not being still. You've treated me all day, now it's my turn to treat you."

Ophelia slid her tongue down his neck, breathing in the scent of his sweat mixed with his new Jimmy Choo cologne. She swirled her tongue around his hairy nipple and pinched it with her lips. Marco leaned his head back and moaned.

Her hair pooled in his lap as she kissed her way down his hard abs and swirled her tongue in his belly button. She followed the dark path of hair from his belly button to the top of his boxers. His underwear was sticking up like a circus tent and she could see a couple dark spots of pre-cum excitement. She gave him kisses on his warm flesh atop the waistline of his boxers from one hip to the other.

She looked up at him and gave him a wicked smile as she curled her fingers along his waistband and pulled them down over his rigid cock. Marco lifted his ass off the bed as she pulled on the boxers and slid them down his legs and tossed them to the floor.

Ophelia ran her hands up each of his legs until they met at his groin and she took his cock in both fists. Her pink tongue slid out of her mouth and she swirled it around the bulbous head of his cock. She then sucked him into her mouth, her lips sliding down his shaft until they touched her hands still gripping him.

"Ooh," Marco moaned as her head began bobbing up and down on his cock. He spread his legs slightly and one of Ophelia's hands moved down to cup and fondle his balls while her other hand stroked his cock in rhythm with her mouth.

The pressure was building inside Marco and he knew he could explode any moment if he wanted to. But there was no way he wanted this to end so quickly. He let his body revel in the glorious sensation she was providing but he let his mind drift to earlier in the night, replaying the scene in his head of when he'd found Rory Stanton walking alone toward Le Rogue hotel.

Stanton had been at the restaurant Lexy not far from the French Quarter, dining with a beautiful redhead. When they'd left the restaurant, Marco was surprised to see Stanton walk the woman to a cab. He kissed her on the lips and then the neck. Marco was pretty certain he'd read her lips to say 'I'll see you in a bit' before the taxi's door closed.

"I said to be still," Ophelia said as Marco pulled her off of him and rolled her onto her back on the bed.

"I can't take any more," he growled in her ear as his hand jerked her white G-string down to her knees and she kicked them off the rest of the way. Ophelia giggled as he got on top of her and she wrapped her arms around his strong back. His throbbing cock pierced her cunt and she moaned something in her native tongue as she raised her ass and spread her legs while he filled her.

Marco had followed Stanton almost four blocks, still with no intention of taking him out tonight but always prepared in his line of work for any eventuality. Stanton turned a corner that led to Le Rogue and there was not a moving person or car in sight. Marco slipped the six-inch stiletto into his left hand and quickened his pace behind the man.

His soft-soled shoes didn't make so much as a whisper and when he was directly behind his target, Marco said, "Excusez moi." Stanton, thinking he was alone on the street, spun in surprise. Marco's face was inches from his and his left hand angled upwards just beneath the man's sternum and Marco pressed the button on the stiletto. The blade shot through the man's suit and flesh, rising up underneath his rib cage, nicking his left lung and piercing Stanton's heart.

The man's eyes grew twice as large and his mouth opened to a dark O but no sound came out. Marco could smell the brisket and rice the man had for dinner, as well as a hint of the redhead's perfume still on his lips, flowery and powdery. Marco eased the man to a sitting position against the wall and pulled his knife free, swiping the blood on Stanton's jacket before retracting the blade and disappearing in the shadows. Driving away shortly thereafter the knife was tossed from the Porsche into a passing river, along with his gloves.

"Marco!" Ophelia screamed out as he continued furiously fucking her, his face inches above her smelling her perfume, her cinnamon toothpaste, her Appletini. Her mouth opened to an O and she cried out in ecstasy and arched her back as tidal waves roared through her body causing her to shiver and shake.

"Oh! Oh! Oh!" she cried.

"Look at me," Marco grunted, his lips pulled back from his teeth.

Ophelia's jaw quivered as she met Marco's eyes and he unleashed himself inside her and her body exploded in unison. He kept thrusting, squeezing out all of him into her as she dug her nails into his back and had no control over the spasms of her body. Even after he had pulled out of her and they lay side by side, her head against his shoulder, her body was racked with aftershocks.

"What was that?" Ophelia said dreamily.

"You've had orgasms before," he replied with a smile.

"Not so many, so intense. It's like I've died and gone to heaven."

"La petite mort," Marco said.

"What's that?"

"The little death. What the French call orgasms."

"Oh yeah, you've told me that before. Well, if that's what death feels like, we've got nothing to fear."

# CHAPTER 4

"Don't be afraid," Evan said standing beside his couch and looking down at the girl whose body was covered with a rainbow-striped sheet.

"I'm not afraid of you," she replied. "But I would like to know why the fuck I'm naked."

"You're not naked. You've still got your bra and panties."

"Panties, I hate that word. They're underwear."

"Okay. But you've still got them on."

"And you took off the rest of my clothes?"

"Well, yeah, I had to."

"Uh-huh. I suppose you just had to jerk off on me, too, didn't you?"

"What? No!" Evan said shocked.

"I know what jizz smells like, that ammonia stench. And I already know what a perv you are."

"I'm glad you're a jizz expert, but you know what else smells like ammonia? Ammonia. It's from cleaning your blood off my floor."

She tried to sit up on the couch but that was quickly overcome with dizziness and she lay back down.

"Take it easy, you lost a lot of blood."

"I feel like I've been drugged."

"I did give you some anesthesia and a mild sedative."

"You fucking drugged me? Are you kidding me? What, am I like your sex slave now you fucking sicko?"

"It was necessary so I could sew you up."

"Sew me up? What the fuck are you talking about? Did you take out my kidney or something and sell it on the black market?"

"Your leg, remember?" Evan said pointing at the sheet mid body.

She pulled the sheet down. Her large breasts were held close together in a plain evergreen bra and her cotton underwear were white and yellow striped. Evan always assumed women were fanatical about matching their bra and panties, but obviously that wasn't so important to this girl. A white patch of gauze bandages about three inches square was taped to the inside of her left thigh. Evan's eyes were staring four inches above the bandage at her underwear that must have ridden up while she slept and he could now see the indent of her pussy slit molded into the fabric.

"No, don't touch it," Evan told her as she reached for the bandage.

"I want to see what the fuck you mean you sewed me up."

"I was a pre-med student, I know what I'm doing. Trust me, it's fine and you shouldn't mess with it."

She stopped and looked at him. "You're a doctor?"

"I was going to school to become a doctor."

"Let me guess, an ob-gyn?"

"Very funny. No, an ER surgeon."

"So you've done this before?" she asked motioning to her leg.

"Well, sort of. Not on a human."

"What's that fucking mean?"

"We'd practice on pig skins."

"Oh great," she said and let her head plop back down on the pillow. She reached for the sheet and pulled it over her. "So now my leg's going to look like a football."

"I aced that class. If it heals properly you'll barely be able to see the scar."

"What do you mean it if heals properly? I don't like being some Bride of Frankenstein. Where am I? This doesn't look like any hospital room I've ever been in before."

"It's my apartment."

"Why didn't you bring me to the hospital?"

"Because I remembered you telling me you didn't want to go to jail."

"When did I say that?"

"When, um, after you said I could frisk you."

She shook her head. "Why were you chasing me if that wasn't your house?"

Evan shrugged. He didn't have a good answer for that.

"What were you doing in that house?" she asked.

Evan looked around his living room thinking of a good lie or story he could tell, but then decided what the hell, he had nothing to lose telling the truth. "I was there to burglarize the place."

"I thought you lived there. You had a key and I heard you come in the front door. And then you went straight to the bathroom."

Evan's cheeks reddened.

"I saw you sneaking out of the room," Evan said, "and I thought maybe you lived there and was going to call the police or something. When I ran out of the house and saw you running I just took off after you. I guess I wasn't even sure what I was thinking. Do you do that a lot?"

"What?"

"Burglarize people's houses?"

"I do what I have to when I need to," she replied.

"How long have you been doing it?"

"What's with all the questions? If I wanted to be interrogated I'd turn myself into the police."

"I'm not interrogating you, I'm just asking questions."

"That's pretty much the definition of interrogation, college boy."

"I'm just curious. I mean, aren't you curious about me and what I was doing there?"

"Not really. What I'm curious about is where are my clothes?"

"Gone."

"What do you mean 'gone'?"

"I had to cut them off of you. Your pants were ruined anyway from the fence and all the blood."

"That doesn't explain my shirt."

"I tried to take it off you but it was too tight." As he said it out loud he realized it didn't sound so good.

"And why on god's green earth did you feel the need to take off my shirt other than for your own perverted pleasure?"

"Well, because your pants were off I didn't want you to get cold so I turned the heat up but then with that long sleeved tight shirt I was afraid you'd overheat so I thought it best to equalize your body."

"Equalize my body? Is that something you learned in pre-med?"

"No, it just made sense at the time."

"What time is it?"

Evan looked to the kitchen where a diamond shaped clock hung on the wall. "A little after three."

"In the afternoon?" Evan nodded his head. "Oh shit, I've got to go. If my car gets towed--"

"I've got it."

"Got what?"

"I found the key fob in your pocket and after I fixed you up I went looking for your car."

"Wait, how would you know what my car even looked like?"

"I didn't. But I know the area and you obviously weren't parked in the gated community and the apartment complexes surrounding the neighborhood all require stickers on the windows or they'll get towed. So I rightly assumed you parked at one of the strip malls."

"But I didn't park at a strip mall."

"I know, you were even smarter than I thought when I found your car at the Logan Theater Cineplex parking lot."

"But how did you find my car?"

"I just kept pushing the 'Panic' button on the key fob until it set off one of the cars," Evan said. "Who's Charlie?"

"What?"

"The registration in the glove box is to Charlie Bonner. So that's obviously the owner of the car. Did you steal it?"

"I'm Charlie," she said. "Can we skip with the interrogation? My head hurts. And I need to go to the bathroom."

"I don't have a bedpan," Evan told her, "but I could bring you a frying pan."

"I'm not peeing in a fucking frying pan. Help me to the bathroom."

"You need to stay off that leg."

"That's why I said for you to help me."

"Um, okay."

Charlie sat up and immediately felt dizzy.

"You've got to go slow," Evan told her. "Do you want me to carry you?"

"I don't think you're that strong."

"It's not like you're that fat or anything."

"Who said anything about me being fat?" she said defensively.

"No, I said you're not fat. Just let me carry you. I carried you here, didn't I?"

"I don't know what you did to me while I was out."

Evan bent down and carefully slipped an arm under her knees and the other around her back under her armpits. "I didn't do anything except save your life."

"And tear off my clothes."

"Again, part of saving your life. Here we go," he said and lifted her off the couch.

"Hey! Watch the hand on my tit."

"I'm not grabbing your tit. I'm just keeping you from falling."

She put her arm around his shoulder and he readjusted his hand so it wasn't so close to her breast. He carried her across the hardwood floor of the living room and then had to walk sideways down the hallway to the bathroom door. He squeezed her close to him, her breasts and hips pressed close against him to get through the bathroom door and then he set her gently atop the toilet seat. He stood there looking at her.

"I think I can manage from here," she told him.

"Oh, right." Evan stepped outside the bathroom door and closed it behind him.

Charlie put her weight on her good leg and tried to stand but couldn't. She kept seeing little black dots in her vision and feeling light headed. "Hey," she called out.

"Yeah?" Evan said from the other side of the door.

"Are you just standing on the other side of the door listening to me?"

"Well, yeah, in case you needed my help."

"You perv."

"Sorry. I can give you some privacy."

"No, I need your help."

Evan opened the door. Charlie put an arm around his shoulder and he balanced her with one arm and lifted the toilet lid with the other and then set her down on the seat.

"Do you want me to, uh," he looked at her underwear.

"No, perv Griffin, I got it from here. And don't stand outside the door this time. That's just creepy."

"No it's not. It's being an attentive doctor."

"They teach that in pre-med, or is that just another thing you made up yourself?"

"You know," Evan said as he exited the bathroom, "you could be a little more grateful."

# CHAPTER 5

"No, no, I'm grateful," Nanae said having already stuffed the little baggie of meth into her jeans pocket. "But I was also hoping for, you know, a little money. I've got bills and stuff, too."

"If you need money," Fox told her, "then sell the dope. Or do what you do best."

"I'm taking a break. I've got a little problem down there."

They were standing in a Burger King bathroom, the door locked behind them. Nanae was wearing a pair of jeans so skinny Fox wouldn't be able to pull them up even one of his legs. She had a partially buttoned white blouse that showed most of her blue bra. Fox was wearing his usual Khakis, a plain gray Polo shirt and a light jacket.

"Problem?" Fox said. "Girl, I swear if you've given me any sort of disease--"

"Not that sort of problem. It's a ruptured cyst."

"What's that mean?"

"It means it hurts like hell and I'm probably going to need surgery. And I don't have insurance."

"Your mouth still works, right?"

"Fox, sometimes you're a real..."

"What? Say it."

"Nothing," she said and looked down at the dirty white tiles.

"Tell you what," Fox said. "If this info on Hilo pans out I'll throw a little something extra your way." He had no intention of giving her anything more without receiving something more in return, but he saw she welcomed the sentiment.

"Okay," she replied, never fully believing anything the cop told her. But she knew it was better to have him as a friend rather than an enemy. She looked at Fox and then his crotch and asked, "Do you want me to?"

He gave it a moment's thought and he never liked turning down an opportunity to get a nut off, but he knew he had to run with this info while it was still hot. "Next time," Fox told her and exited the restroom.

The short, chubby black man had a cock about the length and width of a bottle of cola. He was putting it to use fucking an ugly Asian chick from behind. She was a thick girl, though not as thick as him, and she was on the bed with her ass up and her face down. Her small breasts shimmied like scoops of pudding in an earthquake as she was pounded repeatedly.

His cock felt amazing and she knew her pussy would be sore for days. She wondered briefly if she thought she could take him in her ass, but then discarded that idea for fear she'd never get her asshole to close normally again. It practically felt like he was ripping her in two as it was and she screamed out with every thrust.

He'd been fucking the shit out of her for almost twenty minutes but he wasn't feeling anywhere close to ejaculating. He wasn't about to stop until he got off and he shut his eyes and thought about the Victoria's Secret runway show that was on TV a couple nights ago. Of course it was a little hard to concentrate with this girl screaming as if she was being murdered. He was glad he'd recently moved out of the apartment to this house because it kept the neighbor's complaints down.

Loud banging came from the other room and at first he thought it was someone banging on the wall. He continued banging the Asian chick. Then it struck him like a flash of lightning that no one should be banging on his walls because he wasn't in an apartment or hotel.

"Oh fuck!" he yelled as he pulled his glistening cock free from her sloppy pussy and he dove for the SKS assault rifle propped next to the bed.

His bedroom door burst open, wobbling precariously as it came off two of its hinges.

Standing naked beside the bed, his cock dripping a slimy stream to the carpet, he leveled the gun at the figure barreling through the doorway.

Fox dove as if sacking a quarterback, catching the naked black man around the shoulders and slamming him into the wall. The rifle went off harmlessly into the ceiling and luckily it wasn't fully auto so it was only a single round. Hansel was right behind Fox through the door and he tackled the naked Asian lady on the bed. Sergeant was right behind the two and helped Fox handcuff the portly guy.
"How's it going, Hilo?" Sergeant said.

Ten minutes later Hilo was sitting in a chair next to the dining room table. His hands were handcuffed behind his back and he had a red towel wrapped around his waist. The Asian, Suzy, was wearing an oversized robe and sat handcuffed in the living room on the couch.
Sergeant was sitting on a chair in front of Hilo and Fox was standing beside him with his arms crossed. Cole was standing in the living room watching Suzy while Hansel and Winters continued their search of the house. On the dining room table were two small baggies of meth and a gallon Ziploc with some mid level weed.
"This is bullshit," Hilo said, "you don't even have a warrant."
"We heard someone screaming for their life," Fox said. "That's probable cause."
"That won't hold in court," Hilo spat.
"PC or no PC, you took a shot at one of my officers," Sergeant said. "Attempted murder of a police officer will get you life."
"How did I know you were cops?" Hilo said looking from Fox to Sergeant. "It was self defense. I thought you were home invaders. I didn't hear anyone saying police."
Sergeant shook his head. "You and your attorney can argue with the DA if you want. But I'll be honest with you, we're not here for you."

Hilo looked at the girl in the living room and then the cops before saying, "Man, I ain't no snitch. I got nothing to say about anybody." He spoke extra loud so Suzy was sure to hear him.

Sergeant called out to Cole, "Get her dressed and take her out to the car." Cole lifted her by her arm and led her into the bedroom. Sergeant turned to Hilo and then looked at the drugs on the table. "Looks like we got, what, a couple of eight balls of meth and half a pound of dro."

Hilo looked at the drugs on the table and had an idea what was going on. He had at least ten ounces of meth in his bedroom along with around thirty grand in cash, but it's not like he could argue those points to the cop in front of him. No criminal in his right mind is going to try to convince a judge that he had more drugs than he had been charged with.

"I've got a medicinal prescription," Hilo said.

"I didn't know they were giving those out now for meth," Fox said.

"With this petty shit on the table," Sergeant said, "I'm pretty sure a good attorney could get it thrown out. But if we were to find more drugs or add the gun charge the feds would likely pick it up and you'd be looking at twenty-five as an armed career criminal, Hilo. Not to mention firing at one of my officers."

Hilo looked over Sergeant's shoulder as Cole led Suzy out of the house. "What do you want from me, man?"

"Casablanca," Sergeant said.

Hilo looked at him stone faced.

"Don't act like you don't know who I'm talking about."

"I won't testify on no stand," Hilo said as he looked away.

"Does it look like we want to do paperwork?"

"So, I tell you where to find Casablanca and all this goes away?" he asked motioning to the dining room table.

Sergeant shook his head. "No, you tell us what we want to know about him and you get charged with this bullshit. We've got to justify kicking in your door. Besides, we just let you walk and what's Suzy going to tell people?"

Hilo looked down at his bare feet. "So my guns and the rest of my dope?"

"Don't know what you're talking about," Sergeant said.

"And my thirty bands?"

"Doesn't ring a bell."

"You is all on some dirty shit."

"No, Hilo," Fox said, "if it had been anyone other than us you'd be going away for a long ass time. You should be thanking us."

"Yeah, right. Why don't you whip out your dick and piss on me and tell me it's raining."

The rain wasn't much more than a misting as Fox got out of his Charger and walked into The Backdoor. It was a small strip club on the west side of town with no more than eight girls working at any one time. It was a rundown place in need of new everything, including girls. Most of the strippers came here when they could no longer get hired at any of the other clubs.

Fox wasn't a big strip club guy but then he wasn't here for a lap dance. "Is Sasha here?" he asked the bartender after ordering a beer. The bartender reminded him of Yogi Bear.

"Yeah," Yogi said.

"Do you know where she is?"

The bartender shrugged.

"You've been a great help," Fox said and turned his back to the bar.

The strip club didn't have a stage but rather a pole in the center of the club with a brass railing circling it to give the stripper room to swing her arms and legs without smacking one of the patrons in the head. A blonde with nice fake tits and a saggy ass was making moves half-heartedly on the pole while three guys watched.

On the other side of the club were four small couches against the wall, two of them with guys getting lap dances. Small cocktail tables, each with two shoddy metal and fabric chairs, were spread throughout the club. Two strippers, one in a gold bikini and other in a black corset, sat at one of the tables, both of them immersed in their cell phones.

Fox approached and neither looked up. "Excuse me," he said.

The lady in the corset looked up disinterested and asked, "You want a dance?"

"I'm looking for Sasha."

"Don't know her," the other girl said without looking up.

"I think she's in back," the first lady replied and put her head back down to her phone.

Fox walked to a door alongside the bathrooms marked *Employees Only*. He went inside. It was a small changing room not more than ten feet square with wooden benches along one wall and lockers along another. A third wall had a cluttered counter top and mirrors on the wall.

Sasha was bent over with her ass pointed at the mirrors and she was looking over her shoulder at herself. She was wearing a white thong and a white and red striped bra that made Fox think of candy canes. She had shoulder length yellow hair that was curled like corkscrews.

"Doing a backdoor inspection?" Fox asked.

She glanced at him in the mirror and said, "Some creep bit me on my ass. I can't tell if the mark is still there."

"Need some help?"

She smiled at him and said, "Always the helper, huh?"

"You know me, to protect and serve."

"Uh-huh."

He approached and touched her ass cheek. "Yeah, there's a mark."

"Ow! Don't touch it."

"Those are words no guy wants to hear in a strip club."

"Very funny," Sasha said as she stood up. She was the same height as Fox. "What are you doing here?"

"I've come to rescue you. I've got six grand burning a hole in my pocket. Thought you might like to go to the casino."

Sasha chewed on her lip thinking it over. Fox pulled out his cut from the Hilo job and showed it to her. There would still be another couple grand from the dope once Hansel moved it through his source in the bay area.

"Do I get to keep what I win?" Sasha asked. "Or are we just going for fun?"

"Both."

"And after?"

Fox shrugged. "We'll see how lucky we are."

"I've got to pay the house fee of sixty bucks if I leave early," she told him.

Fox handed her three twenties.

"And I've got to tip the bartender and DJ."

He gave her two more twenties.

"And--"

"Don't push it," Fox said and slapped her on the ass.

"Ow! Not on my sore spot."

"Get dressed and let's go."

# CHAPTER 6

"When do we leave?" Ophelia asked.

"As soon as you're packed," Marco said.

"You got tickets for us already?"

"Something like that."

Ophelia smiled and gave him a kiss on the cheek and went into the large walk in closet. "How long will we be gone?"

"A few days tops."

Marco liked that she was her own boss, operating some sort of Internet drop shipment business. It gave her the flexibility to travel at any time. Any other woman he had been with always had to juggle her work schedule when he wanted to take her on a vacation, which he liked to take a lot. Of course this was a business trip and the first time he had ever brought someone with him when he was going to do a job. He knew it wasn't a wise decision but he couldn't help himself because he more than enjoyed her company, he liked being in her essence. His thoughts and feelings with her were unlike anything he'd ever before experienced or even imagined were possible. This was going to be a trip of many firsts.

"I've never been to Minnesota," Ophelia said from the closet.

"Me neither."

"Will it be cold?"

"Probably."

"So I should wear more than this?" she asked stepping out of the closet wearing only a smile.

"Maybe a hat," Marco said as he stepped towards her. He cupped one hand over her pussy and his other hand went to the back of her head and he pulled her mouth to his. Their breath became one as their tongues danced and he could feel the small landing strip above her clit tickling his palm.

"This is so fun!" Ophelia said as she looked out the window at the small landing strip disappearing beneath them. She had never flown in a small personal aircraft and she loved the feeling of the butterflies in her stomach. She was beside Marco in the co-pilot seat and both of them were wearing bulky headsets with a microphone situated in front of their mouths.

They were flying in Marco's Van RV-10, a four-person airplane that he had built himself from a kit over a six-month period. It was a two-tone white and brown craft with a fuel capacity of a thousand nautical miles, which was a little over eleven hundred and fifty miles on a topographical map of the United States. Their destination was under a thousand miles away, so he could make it without having to stop to refuel.

"How fast are we going?" Ophelia asked after Marco had gone through his checklist and had set the autopilot on its course once they'd reached around eleven thousand feet.

"About as fast as she'll go," Marco replied. "A hundred and seventy knots."

"What's a knot?"

"One point one five oh eight miles per hour."

"Huh?"

"It means we're doing about a hundred and ninety five miles an hour."

"Why didn't you just say that?" she asked with a smile. "How long until we're there?"

"The skies are clear and we're not dealing with any headwinds, so ETA is five hours, or around twenty-two hundred hours."

"Ten o'clock," Ophelia said.

"Very good."

"I was married to a military man."

"Thankfully he wasn't a very smart man to have let you go," Marco said and then to get off that topic he pointed towards the west. "Look at that sunset."

"So beautiful," Ophelia said leaning forward. She looked at Marco. "Thank you."

"For what?"

"Bringing me with you. I know you've said once before that you always took your business trips alone."

"I didn't like the thought of being away from you for three days." Since Ophelia had returned from her cruise a couple months ago Marco hadn't let more than two days pass without seeing her and after two weeks he'd moved her into his town home and only once was gone for more than twenty-four hours taking care of a job. Truth be told, he had more than enough money earned not just from his assassination fees but also due to the fact that he received his payments in crypto currencies, some of which had increased more than nine hundred percent in value, making Marco worth over a hundred million dollars. He pondered what it would be to retire with this beautiful woman and simply live the good life of travel and leisure.

"Are we more than a mile in the sky?" Ophelia asked. Everything on the ground looked like little kids' toys.

"We're actually above two miles."

"Want to join the two mile high club?" she asked.

Marco smiled. "It would be a little tricky. And dangerous."

"How dangerous?"

"Not that much," he lied. The autopilot was already set and he didn't need to concern himself with avoiding any Class B airspace over any major cities from New Orleans to the outskirts of Minneapolis. With the route he had chosen he was actually able to make the entire flight without having to communicate with anyone on the ground, nor had he filed any flight plan, so for all intents and purposes the plane didn't exist.

Of course what he had in mind now with Ophelia would violate multiple FAA regulations and would undoubtedly mean the loss of his pilot's license if found out, but there was little chance of that happening. And when you weighed those violations with what he was flying to Minnesota to do, they suddenly seemed rather paltry.

"So how do we do this?" Ophelia asked with bubbly excitement as she undid her seatbelt.

"I've never done it before. We should probably get in the back seats so we don't hit any of the controls."

"Okay," she said and turned to climb between the two front seats to the back.

"Hold on," Marco said at the same time her head jerked the communication plug out of the control panel. "You've got to take off your headset."

"Oh, sorry," she giggled and pulled the headphones off. She set them on the seat and then began to climb over the front seats. She was wearing a white dress with golden spirals and her hip bumped Marco's shoulder. He slipped a hand up her skirt and rubbed her ass.

"What are you doing?" she asked playfully.

"Helping."

"Me or yourself?"

"Yes."

Ophelia wiggled her ass and then she was falling into the back seats laughing.

"Are you okay?" Marco asked.

"I don't know if you'll be able to make it over those seats," she said.

"I'm pretty flexible."

"You are," she agreed having watched him do his morning tai chi routines that were so slow and fluid that it looked like he was moving underwater.

"Are you ready?" he asked as he began unbuttoning his teal colored shirt. He unclasped his seatbelt.

"Do you mean am I naked?"

"That's exactly what I mean."

"Almost," she giggled.

Marco set his shirt on the co-pilot seat and then undid his belt and pants. He was already getting hard just thinking about what was about to take place. He set his charcoal grey pants atop his shirt and set his grey silk boxers atop the pile. He made a final check of all the plane's gauges and the autopilot before removing his headset.

He turned in his seat and froze. There was enough twilight to see Ophelia perfectly and his cock shot to full attention at the sight. She had one of her legs propped against the fuselage and her other pressed against a seat back, her legs spread and her pussy bared to Marco. She was completely naked and had a mischievous grin as the fingers of one hand were rubbing her pussy and the other squeezing one of her breasts.

"Are you coming?" she asked.

"Keep that up and I'll be coming before I even get there."

"Do you need help?"

"No, you keep doing what you're doing."

He could feel his heartbeat in his cock as he began to make his way over the seats. He was careful not to let his feet hit any of the controls behind him as he went head first into the backseat.

Ophelia squealed and laughed when his head came down on her chest. She cupped his head in her hand as his mouth found one of her voluptuous breasts and her pebble hard nipple that he sucked between his lips. Her other hand slid across his suspended torso until she came to his hardened manhood hanging down like a stalactite. It was even dripping like one and she smeared the pre-cum with her thumb.

"Come on, lover, get back here," she said and pulled on his member.

"Be careful with the joystick," he said as he eased himself the rest of the way into the back, his body falling against Ophelia's. His cock pressed against Ophelia's abdomen.

"Almost a hole in one," she said. "Here, let me help."

Marco shifted his hips as she guided his cock to the glory hole between her legs. Her pussy was slick and tight and she spread her thighs even further apart as she welcomed him in.

"Oh yes," she moaned as his cock pushed into her and filled her. "Oh, my, yes."

He groaned in satisfaction as he sunk fully into her pink warmth. His chest pressed against her breasts as he leaned forward and their mouths came together. His tongue played with her lips, licking the top one and then around to the bottom. Her mouth parted and he pushed into her, searching, tasting, longing.

He pulled his hips back slowly, her bright pink pussy lips squeezed tight around his shaft. He pulled out until only the head of his cock was still in her and then he pushed back into her wanting pussy. Ophelia moaned in his mouth as he grinded his pelvis against hers. Her hands moved up and down his back and over his ass as he began to slowly and deeply fuck her.

He had one hand behind her lower back and his other hand was in a fist in her hair as he continued kissing her, giving her his breath, his life. She lifted her hips to meet his thrusts and he loved how perfectly their bodies fit together. With each thrust he felt her nipples rubbing up and down against his chest.

"Oh Marco," Ophelia moaned dreamily when he finally pulled his mouth away. His hips were moving faster and they could feel the small plane shuddering beneath them, the sound of the single engine loud in the cockpit. "Oh Marco, I love you, Marco."

"I love you, too," he said, surprising himself when the words came out so easily.

"Marco!" she cried.

"Ophelia!" he grunted.

"Marco!" and then she was screaming like one of the Bee Gees singing 'Staying Alive.' Her body felt like a Fourth of July sparkler that had been lit and she screamed louder, drowning out the plane's engine. She dug her nails into Marco's back as his cock flew in and out of her like an engine piston.

He threw his head back and yelled and then hit the ceiling with a loud thump. The plane bounced slightly as his man juices surged through him and it felt like rockets taking off out of the head of his cock as he continued pumping furiously against her beautiful body.

When he finally settled down, his body meshed against hers, her legs wrapped around his waist, he thought about what he'd said. "I mean it, what I said," he told her breathlessly in her ear.

"I know," she said as her fingers moved like floating feathers up and down his back. "Your actions have been louder than words."

He pushed himself up with a hand on the chair so he could look at her face. His cock was still buried inside her and he could feel small pulses every now and then, not sure if they were from him or her. It was dark now with only a light glow coming from the controls and navigation screens at the front of the plane. It was still enough to see the glimmer in her eyes.

After almost a minute of staring, Ophelia asked, "What?"

"You're the one," he told her.

"The one what?"

"The one I'm going to marry."

"Are you asking me?"

He shook his head slightly. "Not yet. I'll do it proper when I do."

She smiled and he kissed her deeply.

They landed at a desolate airfield in Farmington, Minnesota, about thirty minutes southeast of Minneapolis. There were closer airports he could have flown to but he preferred the smaller, unmanned airfield so there was no record of his comings and goings. He had rented an empty hangar at the airport using an online service and he filled up his plane using prepaid credit cards before pushing the plane in the hangar. It was always good to be ready to leave at a moment's notice.

The greatest benefit by far of flying his own plane to such unmanned fields was having the freedom to travel with his tools of the trade without hassles. He carried a .308 sniper rifle with a sound suppressor that was disassembled in three pieces in a locked briefcase. In his travel bag were his clothes, hygiene items and his 9mm H&K compact pistol in a small of the back holster. In his suit coat was a new six-inch stiletto and a new throw away smart phone, which he brought to life.

"What now?" Ophelia asked.

Fifteen minutes later a white Chevy Malibu arrived. Their Uber driver took them to a nice two-story home with a four-car garage on the bluffs of west Bloomington. "Oh my god, look at the view," Ophelia said as she looked out the large living room windows at the river valley below.

"It's beautiful," Marco replied looking at her from behind. He hugged her from behind, his hands on her abdomen and pulling him into her. "Let's order us some pizza. What do you like?"

"Is this house yours?" she asked.

"It's a vacation rental. I prefer real houses over hotels." He didn't tell her that the reason was because he could do it all online with fake data - it didn't matter as long as the credit cards went through - and he didn't have to deal with front desks, cameras, housekeeping, guests, or anyone knowing his comings and goings. He'd always rent the vacation properties for a full week, even though he only planned to use the place for three days. This way no one could ever pinpoint when and where he was with any certainty, that is if they were even able to figure out what name he rented it under. Security was first and foremost in his line of work.

He wondered if he'd still take all of these precautions if he decided to get out of his line of work. He was pretty sure he would because it had become a way of life - he didn't think he'd ever be able to fully relax, he always had to be ready for anything, never let life catch him by surprise.

"What are you thinking about?" Ophelia asked as she rubbed her ass against his groin as they stood looking at each other in the reflection of the living room window.

"Surprises," he told her.

She smiled thinking he was talking about a marriage proposal surprise. She was surprised herself because she was actually welcoming the idea, which also scared her because she hadn't even been out of her last marriage for more than a year. She had been feeling like she was damaged goods, had been through a lot of emotional abuse with her ex-husband, and told herself she was taking a long hiatus from men and dating. But then Marco had approached her at the pastry shop in Miami and waited there for a week, and he'd put her on a pedestal ever since. It sometimes felt too good to be true and she feared falling from the pedestal. She didn't want to disappoint Marco.

"How long will it take the pizza to get here?" she asked.

"I haven't ordered it yet. Why, do you want to get a quickie in?"

She turned in his arms and faced him. "I want to take a shower and then we'll eat and then we'll make passionate, slow love."

# CHAPTER 7

"Put it in slowly. There you go. Can you feel that? Now slide it back and forth. Faster now. Ease up on the pressure. Ooh, yeah. Aha! There it is."

He couldn't believe it, he'd done it. A warm flush flooded through his body as Evan looked at Charlie. She smiled and nodded her head. "You can pull it out now," she told him.

Evan removed the small metal rake from the keyhole and then finished turning the torsion bar until he heard and felt the deadbolt disengage. He had picked his first lock and couldn't believe how easy it was.

"See? I told you," Charlie said.

Evan stood next to his open apartment door with his mouth slightly ajar. "I got to try that again," he said and reached his hand around the door and locked it, the deadbolt poking out the edge of the wooden door. He slipped the two metal tools into the keyhole and bent his face toward the lock.

"There's nothing to see," Charlie said, "it's all about feeling the pins against the rake. Stand up straight or you'll look suspicious to anyone who might look your way. There you go. No, don't look down at your hands. You need to be watching your surroundings using your periphery to make sure no one is observing you or giving you more than a passing glance. If you're in a busy area, such as an apartment complex, you should hold a set of keys in your hand and if someone comes you can act like you're just locking the door, give the keys a jingle and casually walk away."

"What if it's the homeowner?" Evan asked as his fingers attempted to manipulate the lock while he looked at Charlie.

She was sitting on his couch in some jeans and a t-shirt eating a pint of Ben and Jerry's Cherry Garcia while watching Evan.

"You either run or have a good story," she said with a mouth full of ice cream.

"A story? Oh, sorry, I was trying to break into your house."

"If you haven't unlocked the door yet, you've technically done nothing wrong. All they saw was you with a set of keys in your hand. So tell them you have the wrong house, that you were supposed to water your aunt's plants while she was away or your friend from work sent you to pick up his suit for the dry cleaners, or act drunk like you went to the wrong place. You've got to think fast, be ready for anything."

"Got it!" Evan cried excitedly as the keyhole turned and the deadbolt disappeared inside the door. Charlie nodded her head. "I want to try it again, for real," he told her. "Lock the door."

Evan shut his apartment door behind him and Charlie got up from the couch and limped to the door and locked it. Her leg was healing nicely and there was almost no pain now after five days at Evan's. He had brought up her things from her car, what little she had, and when he found out she'd been living out of her ten year old GMC Envoy he insisted she stay with him until she was better. She didn't doubt for a second that he was only doing it in hopes of getting in her pants because she already knew what a perv he was. But it turned out that Evan was actually a pretty nice guy, book smart but street stupid, and they'd had some interesting conversations.

"You never commit crime in the same city you live in," she'd told him when she learned his apartment was less than half a mile from the gated community they had both been burgling. "Haven't you ever heard the saying you don't shit where you sleep?"

"I just figured that if things went bad it would be easier to get away."

"And easier to be identified. And where were your gloves?"

"I don't wear any."

"You're kidding right?"

"This is California, nobody wears gloves," Evan said. "Besides, I've never been in trouble, my prints aren't on file anywhere."

Charlie shook her head. "If you do get caught they'll be able to link you to all of the past crimes that have your prints."

"I heard they don't even take prints from burglaries, not unless there's a bigger crime that happens like murder or something."

"Where'd you hear that?"

"I don't know. A movie, I think."

That's when she learned that most of all of his knowledge about crime and police procedure came from his favorite movies. He was a huge movie buff, especially anything with crime, and she had watched more than a couple of dozen movies with him on his sixty inch 4K flat screen TV in the living room with theater surround sound.

Charlie finished the pint of ice cream in her hands and Evan still hadn't opened the apartment door. She thought maybe he was having trouble but she didn't even hear his tools scraping the lock innards. She looked through the door's peephole and saw Evan, but his back was to the door and he was at the apartment door across from his.

She quickly unlocked the door and swung it open just as she saw the other apartment door swing open. "Evan!" she hissed. "What are you doing?"

He spun around with a Chester Cheetah grin. "I got it!"

"You idiot! What did I tell you about shitting where you sleep?"

"Relax, I'm not doing anything. And I know they don't get home for a few hours."

"Shut and lock that door now!"

"Calm down."

She stood in Evan's doorway with her arms crossed, the empty ice cream carton with a spoon in it dangling from one hand as she looked out over the parking lot to make sure no one paid Evan any mind at his neighbor's door that he was attempting to relock. It was taking him too long and she wanted to snatch the lock picks out of his hands and lock the door for him because she knew she could do it in less than three seconds, as she'd demonstrated on Evan's door earlier when the lock picks had arrived by UPS.

Evan had ordered two identical sets online utilizing second day delivery. He had given her one set to replace the picks she had tossed the other night when running from the home, and the other set he'd kept for himself with the expectation that she'd teach him how to use them.

At first she'd declined until he'd accused her of lying, that she probably never even had any lock picks and surely didn't know how to use them. She had stepped outside his door and told him to lock it and no sooner had he turned the deadbolt knob and it was spinning back to its unlocked position and she opened the door.

"No way!" he said, flabbergasted and thinking maybe he'd not locked the door properly. "I've never seen it done that fast even in a movie."

"That's because movies are fake," she told him not for the first time. "Apartments are especially easy because almost every lock has three or four different keys that will open the door."

"Why does it matter how many keys you have?" Evan asked.

"It's not about how many keys. It's about the multiple pin configurations or combinations that will unlock the door. The property owner might have a master key that works at multiple properties. Then the manager of each property will have a key that only works for all the doors of their complex. And then there will be maintenance keys that will work for only specific wings or areas. Finally there's your own key. So that means you have four times more chances of getting an apartment door open than say a private home that has only a single key combination."

"How do you know all this?"

"I dated a locksmith."

"Was he a burglar?"

"No. That's kind of why it didn't work out."

"Well at least you got something good out of the deal."

Evan finally got the door across the way locked and he returned to his apartment with a shit-eating grin. Charlie turned her back on him and limped to the kitchen to throw away the empty pint container and put her spoon in the sink.

"What are you so mad about?" Evan asked.

"If you're going to do stupid shit like that, don't do it while I'm around. I don't want to go to prison simply because you've got no common sense."

"Don't be so dramatic. It's not like you'd get in any trouble. I was just fooling around. I wanted to see if I really had it. And I did."

"It's serious, Evan," Charlie said glaring at him. "Just possessing those lock picks is a felony charge. And then as soon as you unlocked your neighbor's door that became another felony charge. Felonies mean prison."

Even though Charlie was only nineteen, six years younger than Evan, she sometimes talked and acted like one of his parents. He knew she was overreacting and there was no way he'd actually get in trouble just for unlocking someone's door, especially when he hadn't gone inside and taken anything. And even her getting mad about him not using gloves was ridiculous because it's not like he was doing the burglaries for money.

"What do mean you don't do it for money?" Charlie had asked the first time he had mentioned this.

He kind of shrugged. "I've got money. And my parents are pretty loaded."

"So what are you doing breaking into places?"

"Just to see if I can. And, you know, it's a rush."

"That's about the stupidest thing I've ever heard."

Evan had gone to his bedroom and returned with a shoebox that he opened and showed to Charlie. Inside were a cornucopia of trinkets, none of them of any real monetary value. There were a couple empty key chains, some tie tacks, a few charms, tie clips and single cufflinks.

"What's all this?" Charlie asked, looking but not touching any of it.

"Each item is someplace I've been. A little memento to remind me of the adventure."

"Have you ever been to a psychiatrist?" she asked him.

"Why?"

"Because that's just creepy. You've got problems. You're probably one of those freaks who jerks off in ladies' underwear drawers or shits on their bed. Next thing you know you'll be serial killing people or something."

"I'm not like that. You think you're better than me because you steal people's hard earned money and sentimental jewelry?"

"I do it to survive," she said.

"Because you're too lazy to get a job."

"Lazy? There's nothing lazy about my line of work."

"That's how you look at it?" he asked.

"It's not for everyone."

"So you see yourself like Robin Hood or something?"

"I don't see myself like anyone," Charlie replied. "Robin Hood was an idiot, he gave his loot away. I've been on my own since I was thirteen and I've found what works for me and I don't need to justify it or explain it to anyone, especially someone like you."

"I'm not trying get you mad. I think it's cool what you do. Like that movie with Michelle Pfeifer doing those heists, you know the one, right? Or that Selma Hayek one where she's learning from the master thief. Or how about when Charlize Theron--"

"It's not some pretend movie, okay? This is my life."

"Okay, sorry."

They had sat in silence for a while staring at a crime movie Evan had put on earlier. After a bit he'd asked her what her plan was, if it was just to be a burglar all her life or if there was something she wanted to do.

"I'm not sure," she said. "I had thought about coming to California to join a commune. Maybe find myself or something."

"Really? I think you have to like sex if you're going to join one of those cults."

"I'm not talking about a cult. And what makes you think I don't like sex?"

Evan blushed. "Well...I..." He didn't know what to say.

"Just because I don't want to have sex with you doesn't mean I don't like it."

"What's that supposed to mean? What's wrong with me?"

"You're a pervert."

"I am not a pervert."

"Oh you most certainly are. You proved that the first night we met and you accosted me."

"I didn't accost you. I frisked you only because you said I could."

"Well I thought you were someone else."

"Bullshit. You were willing to do anything to save your ass."

"Not anything," Charlie said.

"I bet. If it was a choice of wearing handcuffs or putting a dick in your mouth, which would you choose?"

"Which would you choose?"

"I'm not sucking some guy's dick!" Evan said.

"Don't be so sure. You keep doing crime the way you do and you'll find yourself in prison. And you're a little too cute for prison. You've got a nice mouth."

"So teach me stuff about crime, about what you know."

"Why would I want to do that?"

"You have to admit I did kind of save your life. I'm a good student." When she didn't respond, he added, "I know of some homes that have a lot of jewelry and when they'll be out of town."

"How do you know that?"

"Like I said, my parents are rich. They have a lot of rich friends."

Charlie shook her head. "You can't commit crimes that can be linked to you in any way."

"No one would ever suspect me. I've never been in trouble."

"Doesn't matter. If you're going to do it right it has to be totally unassociated with your life. You've got a lot to learn."

"So you'll teach me?"

"I don't know. Maybe."

They sat on the couch in silence until Evan asked, "What do you mean I have a cute mouth?"
"Don't be a perv. We're not ever going to fuck."

# CHAPTER 8

"Are you trying to fuck me? Fox asked. "Should I pull my pants down and bend over?"

"You can do whatever you like," the small gray haired man in his seventies said. "Won't change the fact that the watch is fake."

"Turk, if I take this someplace else," Fox said shaking the watch in his hand, "and find out different--"

"There's nothing to find out," Turk told him. "It's a nice looking watch and if it were real I'd be giving you thirty, maybe forty grand. But as it is, it's worth maybe two hundred dollars and I don't buy fakes."

Fox knew the Middle Eastern man was telling him the truth but he didn't want to believe it. He had snatched the watch from Hilo's home, certain that he hadn't been seen doing so, and thought for sure he'd have a little extra bonus in his pocket. It's not like he didn't deserve it, especially being first in the door and almost getting gunned down.

Fox left the back office of the mini mart that Turk owned on the edge of the hood. He got in his Charger and headed to Rusty's for the three o'clock meeting with the crew. On the way he stopped at his stash house in the wealthy northwest suburb.

He had begun renting the single story ranch home less than a year ago when he and the crew had pulled off a few big scores. The place was rented under an assumed name and not even the crew knew about it. Any chance he got he'd skim from their jobs if he could get away with it and he'd never had an issue until their take of some drug mule's jewelry collection and Cole feeling like he'd been cheated. He had been, but there was no way he could ever prove it and the insinuations had created a rift in their relationship. And then on top of that the piece of shit drug mule hired an attorney who got Internal Affairs asking questions about six figures in missing jewelry. They could never prove anything either.

Fox tossed the fake gold and diamond faced watch atop the toilet tank as he took a leak. There was no sense putting it in the safe; he'd trade it off one of these days for a few grams of meth, or maybe even a few ounces if he could convince the sucker it was real.

He got back in his car and as he pulled out of the driveway he swiped his phone app that set the alarm on his place. You could never be too careful these days.

"We've got to be careful," Sergeant said as the five men sat around the poker table. They had drinks and chips in front of them, but they weren't playing cards yet. It was always business before play. Cole had swept the back room of Rusty's for any listening devices or cameras and all the guys knew to keep their phones in their cars.

"IA is investigating at least two reports on us now," Sergeant continued. "I don't think it's enough to start them seriously investigating our assets or putting on surveillance details, but we can't give them anything else to work with. If we do something, it has to be to perfection, no loose ends."

"If we get to Casablanca," Winters said, "it could be our biggest score yet."

"Not if, but when," Fox said.

"I agree," Sergeant said nodding at Fox, "but we're going to take this one slow."

"We still don't know Casablanca's guy," Hansel said. "If we can get him--"

Winters shook his head. "Casablanca could have close to seven figures if we time it right. We don't need his guy."

"But if we find his guy," Hansel explained, "we could take Casablanca down."

"We don't want to take him down," Sergeant said. "We hit him, let him rebuild, and then hit him again for another seven figure payoff. He could be our retirement plan."

"Do we know his places?" Fox asked. "I've got a list of three of his runners and a lead on two more."

"He's got two locations he's working out of," Cole said. "He's also got two homes, different ladies living at each one, but still don't know if he keeps anything there."

"Security?" Sergeant asked.

"He's got an armored BMW, and his two main dudes also drive armored rides." Cole checked his small notepad in front of him. "His two businesses, an auto shop and a plumbing business, have basic alarm systems and the auto shop has two pit bulls on premises twenty four hours."

"I bet that's where he keeps the bulk of his cash," Winters said.

Sergeant shrugged. "No way to know for sure yet. We know he's not going to have his cash and drugs in the same location."

"What if we popped one of his main dudes?" Hansel asked. "We get him to turn and give us the inside scoop."

Fox shook his head. "We don't want to give him any sign or warning that we're on to him."

Winters agreed and added, "Casablanca has been untouchable, but if he thinks it's hot, he could shut down everything before we have a chance to move on him."

"So how will we know when and where to hit?" Cole asked.

"The runners will give us the best read when he's about to re-up," Fox said. "Casablanca lets it get almost dry, driving prices up and everyone scrambling like crazy to get their hands on it before it's all gone. Then he'll come in with a new shipment and the streets are flooded and the runners are going nonstop."

"So once we know when to hit, we still don't know where," Hansel said. "It's not like the five of us can hit four places at the same time."

Sergeant took a drink and then said, "That's why we keep doing our homework and keep a low profile. We can't let Casablanca know we're even sniffing in his direction. If it takes us an extra month or two, so what, it will be worth it. Let's not fuck this one up. This could be the mother lode."

"Plus it wouldn't hurt to not do anything for a month or two," Winters added. "Give IA time to stop snooping around our asses."

"They start snooping around your ass and they'll die of toxic inhalation," Hansel laughed.

"Yeah," Winters retorted, "well they'd need the Jaws of Life to get into your ass."

"What the fuck does that even mean?" Fox asked and the others laughed.

"I don't get it," Hansel said. "You're saying I have a tight ass?"

Cole laughed and shrugged his shoulders saying, "You are sort of a tight ass."

Sasha's ass was tighter than a pocket on a wet pair of skinny jeans. Of course her jeans were around her ankles as Fox stood behind her with his rigid cock pushing between her spread ass cheeks.

"Lube, goddammit!" Sasha screamed.

Fox spit into his hand and pulled the purple head of his cock out of Sasha's asshole. He slathered his palm around the tip of his member and then clasped his hands to her ass cheeks and spread them wide to expose her puckered asshole.

"Ow! Watch out for my bruise!" Sasha whined and Fox moved his hand away from the bite mark on her ass cheek. He pushed his hips forward and the tip of his cock pushed at her asshole and then disappeared into the tightness.

"Slower! Slower!" she yelled.

Fox was getting sick of her complaining and whining and about had a mind to stick his cock in her mouth just to shut her up. But he liked the way her asshole gripped him so tightly and the pressure of her squeezing against his cock as he pushed into her.

"Oh fuck! Ow! Wait!"

Fox pushed into her farther, deeper.

Sasha was clinging to the back of a dining room chair in her small home.

"Fuck! Fuck! Fuck!"

His cock slid into her as his hands spread her ass cheeks apart as far as they'd go. She cried out as his pelvis pushed up against her ass.

"Oh god! Wait!" Sasha pleaded. She was bent over, still wearing her blouse and bra, her breasts heaving for breath. Fox was still wearing his shirt, both of them with their jeans bunched at their ankles, his cock completely swallowed by her tight little asshole.

"I said wait!" Sasha cried as Fox reversed the motion of his hips and began sliding his cock out of her. Her ass was so tight he could feel every ridge and vein of his cock rubbing against the rim of her ass as he pulled back.

"Oh Fox, please!"

He pulled back until only the bulbous head of his cock was still in her, her asshole puckered tightly around him. He couldn't believe how amazing it felt. He only wished she'd shut up so he could enjoy it. He pushed back into her.

"Ow! Wait!"

"Shut the fuck up!" Fox told her.

"What? What did you just-- Aaahh!" she screamed as Fox pulled her hips to him as he thrust his rod fully into her ass.

"Fox!" she cried out as he pulled his cock back.

"Shut!" he said as he rammed into her ass again.

"The fuck!" He rammed into her again.

"Up!" His cock was now pounding into her ass over and over and Sasha made unintelligible cries and yells. Her ass bounced and jiggled with his every thrust and the sound of their bodies clapping together was loud in the small dining room.

The chair she clung to rocked back and forth as Fox fucked her in the ass. She yelled out his name and again begged him to stop. She gasped with surprise and relief when he pulled out of her ass and she fell to her knees, her ass throbbing like it had its own heartbeat.

"I'm sick of all your noise," Fox said as he grabbed her yellow, spiral hair and turned her to face him.

"It was too much," she was saying and then he was shoving his throbbing cock into her mouth. She tried to resist but his grip was tight on her hair and he was pulling her into him.

She thought of bringing her teeth down onto him but he said, as if reading her intentions, "You bite me and you'll be eating out of a straw the rest of your short life."

Sasha wanted to argue or protest or at least say something but she couldn't with his cock sliding in and out of her mouth. A couple times she almost gagged as he hit the back of her throat and streams of spit seeped from her lips and hung from her chin as Fox fucked her face.

Her mouth wasn't as tight as her ass, but it still felt delightful and the only sounds he had to listen to were slurping and gagging sounds as he jerked his hips back and forth faster and faster. His balls bounced against her chin and her head bobbed back and forth, her swollen lips stroking his swollen member. His cock fired off inside her and he clenched his ass cheeks as he ground his pelvis against her face, his warm jizz shooting down her throat. She swallowed all of him until he pulled his dirty cock out of her mouth and then she curled up on the floor and cried.

Fox stepped out of his jeans and went to her bathroom to wash off his sticky member. When he returned to the dining room, Sasha was still on the floor, her pants still around her ankles, and Fox couldn't help but admire the curve of her sweet ass that was facing him.

He got down on the floor beside her and nuzzled his body up against hers, spooning her from behind.

"Fox, no," she said through her tears.

"What? I'm only holding you. There's no reason to be upset. Come on, it's okay," he said as he wrapped his arms around her and hugged her to him. They were both naked from the waist down and she held his arms as he hugged her from behind.

"Why did--"

"Shh," Fox said. "Sometimes you back talk too damn much."

"I was just--"

"Shh. Be quiet and listen to me. There's no one else like you, got that?"

Sasha sniffled and nodded.

"You know everything I do for you, right?"

She nodded again as she clung to his arms wrapped around her chest.

"And do I ask too much in return? Do I?"

She shook her head no.

"I told you I'm going to take you away from that club, right?"

Sasha nodded even though it had been almost eight months since he'd made that promise and she wasn't apt to believe it.

"It's going to happen soon," he told her for the hundredth time. "You do what I say and you can have anything you want. You know that, right? Of course I know what you really want, don't I?"

She felt his hands sliding up under her shirt. His strong hands pushed her bra up and his hands squeezed her tits. She could feel his hardness pressing against the back of her thigh.

"You do want me, don't you?"

She didn't know what she wanted any more other than she knew she didn't want to hurt. She reached her hands between her legs and grasped his hard cock. She guided him toward her pussy so he wouldn't try for her tender ass again.

"That's right," Fox moaned as he slipped his cock into her. Sasha closed her eyes and tried to let herself get lost in his touch.

# CHAPTER 9

Marco was afraid he might be losing his touch. Things couldn't be going more wrong in Minnesota. He knew it wasn't a matter of skill because he was very proficient in what he did. He just wasn't sure his heart was in it anymore; his heart was somewhere else.

The morning after a passionate night of lovemaking, Marco and Ophelia took an Uber to the Mall of America. He gave her a few thousand dollars and told her to have fun and then he took a light rail train to the airport a mile away. Using a false ID and a phony airline-boarding pass he'd printed out in preparation he rented a Toyota Avalon.

Twenty minutes later he was driving through downtown Minneapolis until he found Loring Park. He parked on a side street and took a leisurely stroll through the park and then crossed a couple streets until he reached his target: the Basilica of Saint Mary.

The church was a grand structure with wide steps leading up to a portico overlooking Hennepin Avenue. Marco walked to the top of the steps and looked out over the busy street and beyond. This is where his target would be standing in two days, Saturday. He had already examined the entire area online looking at satellite and street views, but there was nothing better than being able to actually scope out the lay of the land in person. This wasn't a luxury often afforded in his line of work.

Marco watched the heavy traffic on Hennepin Avenue, but on the day of the hit the street would be blocked off and filled with people. On the west side of the basilica was a freeway overpass. Marco looked southward from the top of the steps, past the park that he'd originally walked across to a congested six-lane street that bordered a large art museum. A couple blocks south of that was a six-story apartment building Marco had his eye on, maybe a total of about eight hundred yards away.

The walk took him almost fifteen minutes, waiting at the crosswalks, but when the time came his bullet would travel the distance in less than two seconds. With a couple of simple lock picks he bypassed the apartment building's security door and then used the same tools to unlock the door that led to the roof. Marco was disappointed to see that the rooftop had only a one-foot ledge around the edge of the building, not enough to use for cover. He'd have to utilize Plan B.

Marco left the rooftop, strolled casually down the sixth floor hallway and then departed the apartment building, stopping at the wall of mailboxes and making a couple of mental notes on his way out. He returned to his car and drove around the surrounding streets planning optimal exit strategies and noting street and building cameras to be sure to avoid.

"Where are you going, baby?" Ophelia muttered half asleep. Marco approached the bed fully dressed. He bent down and rubbed Ophelia's ass through the sheets and blankets as he kissed her on the cheek. She smiled.

"Off to work," he told her.

"You'll be back in time for my surprise?" she asked in a dreamy voice.

"Of course I will. There's money on the dresser." He kissed her on the forehead.

"I still have change from yesterday."

"Then you're not trying hard enough." With a final squeeze of her ass he left the room.

Marco drove to a Starbucks in Edina where he utilized the Wi-Fi on a throwaway tablet computer. His Internet search confirmed that Abigail Orr resided in apartment 604 of the building he had been exploring the day before. He also discovered that her husband of forty-seven years, Thomas Orr, had passed away fifteen years ago. Using a throwaway phone, Marco called the number listed to the apartment. After four rings it was answered.

"Mrs. Abigail Orr?" Marco asked in a husky whisper.

"Yes?" replied the squeaky eighty-three year old's voice.

"Of apartment six-oh-four?"

"Yes. Who is this?"

"Standard census count, ma'am," Marco said, keeping his voice low and disguised.

"I can barely hear you," Abigail said, raising her voice.

"Sorry, it must be the connection. Our records show that there are three residents at this address."

"Oh heavens no. It's just me. What is this about?"

"For building records, ma'am. We did have a complaint about your dog."

"What? I've never had a dog. You must be thinking of Mr. Gartenberg in the next-door apartment. Did you know that the other day his two little dogs--"

"We'll make a note of that," Marco told her. "Thank you for your time." He hung up while she continued on with her dog story. Marco put the phone in his pocket, which he disassembled and placed along with the computer in the Faraday bag once back in the car.

His next stop was a Goodwill center in St. Louis Park and then he once again checked and rechecked his routes of egress from the apartment building.

He was done with his work by noon and as much as he'd like to spend the day with Ophelia, he waited until almost four o'clock before returning to the vacation rental where he found his woman waiting with open arms and a smile.

"You made it," she said as they embraced.

"Of course. I'm not going to miss out on this surprise you have for me." He squeezed her body tightly against his.

"Well we still have a couple hours until we have to leave for that," she told him.

"Hmm," Marco said as he let his hands slide down the back of her summer dress and cup her ass. "What shall we do for the next couple of hours?"

"I have an idea or three," Ophelia whispered into his ear before sucking on his earlobe.

Canterbury Park was a horse track and card room in Shakopee, only five miles from the vacation rental but it took nearly forty minutes to finally reach the building through all of the traffic heading to the same location.

"I didn't know it would be so busy," Ophelia said. "Are you excited?"

Marco wasn't, but he didn't let her know. He wasn't a fan of gambling, didn't care for games or sports of chance. He was a man about controlling outcomes and making sure things happen. Ophelia had remembered the chance encounter with Dmitri's wife Maggie and the mention of the men meeting at the track, so she thought it would be fun to see her man in his element and to let him know that she supported his activities.

In truth, Dmitri was the middleman who facilitated many of the hits that Marco did. In the past ten years most of Marco's jobs were done utilizing the dark web to send encrypted target data as well as payments made with crypto currencies. But there were still a number of old school clients who weren't computer savvy and didn't know a crypto currency from an anonymous router and that was where Dmitri came into play. They rarely met at the same place twice and had only met at a racetrack once and that was more than three years ago.

It didn't surprise Marco that Dmitri's wife was in the dark about what her husband did, and Marco was only one shadow of many shady ventures Dmitri was involved with. Obviously Ophelia didn't know what Marco did, and never would, but he was also ready to quit his line of work and try living the happily ever after thing with Ophelia, get married, travel the world, whatever she wanted.

But if there was one thing any successful hitman had to be good at, it was adapting to any situation. So he and Ophelia had a fun time at the track and he let her pick the horses with the funny names and somehow they managed to win more than they lost. He attributed it to her beginner's luck while she was certain it was because of all his track experience with Dmitri.

Saturday morning arrived and Marco was dressed and at the bedside looking down at Ophelia asleep on her back, the blankets only half covering her, one leg sticking out and one beautiful breast bared. He bent down and kissed her nipple.

Ophelia moaned and hugged his head to her breast. "Oh, Marco, what are you doing to me?"

"Anything and everything you want," he told her, his breath warm on her chest. He slid his hand along her exposed thigh and cupped her pussy, nuzzling his palm into her little airstrip. "Be ready to go by two, okay?"

"I'm always ready for you," she said and pushed her pelvis toward his hand.

"I know you are." He kissed her nipple again and gave her pussy a final stroke before leaving the house.

It was almost two hours later before Ophelia got out of bed. She took a long, hot shower and then dressed in a red, silk ruffled designer dress that reached almost to her knees. She had purchased it in a shop at the Mall of America on Thursday and it made her think of leaves on fire. She was standing on the front porch when the yellow Kia from Uber picked her up.

Marco stood outside apartment number 604 with his throwaway cell phone in one hand and a worn and scuffed brown leather briefcase from Goodwill in his other hand. He was wearing a plain dark blue suit and black fedora, both also from Goodwill, along with oversized sunglasses and a thick, well groomed salt and pepper beard. He pressed the call button on the phone and listened to it ring in his ear. A fraction of a second later he could hear a phone ring from within the apartment. It rang again in his ear, then the apartment. After five rings he disconnected the call. As he had assumed, Mrs. Orr was probably at the large gathering at the basilica.

Marco set his briefcase down, placed the phone in his pocket and pulled out his two lock picking tools. He inserted them into the keyhole, manipulated the pins and twenty two seconds later stepped into the apartment after slipping on a pair of clear surgical gloves. He shut and locked the door behind him and set his briefcase on the floor. He stood completely still in the empty apartment, getting a feel for its energy and listening for any possible sounds. Someone was here, he was almost certain of it.

He pulled the new stiletto from his coat pocket and moved through the apartment. Beyond the front door to the left was a small kitchen and dining area, the living room on the right. A hallway ran alongside the kitchen to the left and Marco followed it to the single bedroom with its single bed empty and made. Back in the hallway he stopped at the closed bathroom door. He gripped the knife firmly in his right hand while slowly turning the doorknob with his left.

Marco saw her before she saw him, the naked old lady looking like a shriveled white raisin in the bathtub's plain water. In two steps he was upon her. "Oh!" was all she said before her head was pushed forcefully under the water. Marco held her under with his left hand clasped in her thin blue-gray hair. His right hand held his stiletto needlessly. She didn't thrash so much like a fish but rather wiggled more like a worm for less than thirty seconds before going still.

Marco pulled his hand out of the water and Mrs. Orr's body slid further into the tub, her head tilting back and to the side looking up through lifeless eyes. He dried his hand on a towel beside the tub feeling a little water in the glove of his left hand. He exited the bathroom, shutting the door behind him, and proceeded to the living room, along the way grabbing the small dining room table and dragging it behind him. He placed the table in the middle of the room and adjusted it to line up with one of the living room windows six feet away.

He opened his briefcase and removed the three parts of his sniper rifle, assembling it atop the table, the sound suppressor the last item screwed into place. He extended the bipod legs at the end of the barrel and set the rifle atop the table and then peered through the riflescope.

Satisfied that everything was in order, Marco opened the living room window and returned to the spot behind his rifle, sitting in a chair as he peered through the scope aimed at the basilica eight hundred yards away.

Ophelia had found out online about the recognition ceremony taking place in downtown Minneapolis at the Basilica of Saint Mary. Though her father had been Muslim, when he died her mother remarried an American and became Catholic. Ophelia had enjoyed being a part of the church but had fallen away during her nine-year marriage. She wasn't sure if Marco was religious, though she got the feeling he was maybe spiritual for he always seemed to have a calmness about him.

It was a beautiful day and the basilica was a beautiful church. She wished she could visit inside but that wouldn't be possible as the front portico was roped off for the visiting bishop and the priests that would be getting some sort of awards. The energy of the thousands of people in the streets and all the way back to the park a block away was intoxicating. The crowd grew louder as the large doors of the church opened and the clergy stepped out.

Marco's breathing was steady and controlled as he watched the tiny figures move through the lines of his scope. His heartbeat remained calm and even, just another day at the office. More than a hundred and fifty thousand people would die today across the world, one more added to the list wouldn't make much difference.

His finger rested on the trigger, the butt of the rifle secure against his shoulder, his cheek like a lover's brushing against the side of the stock.

And there he was, the man of the hour, one of the priests to be recognized at the ceremony by the visiting bishop. But obviously this particular priest had fondled the wrong altar boy because Marco's mission parameters had been specific. This hit was to send a message.

As Marco breathed out slowly and his mind sent a message to his trigger finger there came a knock at the door behind him. Marco froze, his first brief thought that Mrs. Orr had somehow lived and crawled out of the tub and was now standing naked behind him, water dripping from her shriveled up body.

He knew that was absurd and he also knew that if someone was knocking at the door, it meant they didn't live there. The knock came again and a squeaky voice on the other side of the door said, "Abigail?"

Marco made a slight adjustment with his rifle and calmly squeezed the trigger. The rifle bucked in his grasp and made a sound no louder than an axe being swung into a tree stump. Through the scope he saw the priest fall forward as if his feet had been swept out from beneath him, the heavy round having hit home in the priest's groin. Though not normally considered a kill shot, Marco was using an explosive tipped round that would tear through the priest's innards like a blender grinding up tomatoes.

Marco didn't watch the priest as he fell down the front of the basilica steps, nor did he pay attention to the collective gasp of thousands of onlookers. His focus instead was on the door behind him, which he heard a key being slid into.

He quickly darted to the kitchen while pulling the stiletto from his pocket. He put his back to the wall as he heard the door open.

"Abigail, is your window open?" asked the little old lady's voice.

The door closed and she moved further into the apartment. There was the sound of only one set of footsteps.

"Abigail, what's your table--"

Marco stepped out of the kitchen, the stiletto driving up under the frail woman's coat and ribcage. Her small brown eyes behind thick glasses looked confused and then content as life left her and she could finally rest forever. Marco pulled the knife out of the old lady and she crumpled to the floor like a dead rope.

With Abigail's drowning, it might have been able to be passed off as accidental or natural causes, but there was no covering up this, even though the only blood was on his knife.

"There was so much blood, it was everywhere," Ophelia said. Marco hugged her shivering body tightly in his arms as they stood in the foyer of the vacation home.

"You should have called me," he said as she buried her head in his chest.

"I wouldn't interrupt your business," she said. "How could someone shoot a priest?" she asked incredulously.

They bleed like every man, Marco thought to himself.

"Are you okay?" he asked.

"I think I'm going to be sick," Ophelia said and broke from his grasp to run to the bathroom.

# CHAPTER 10

Evan rushed to the bathroom, lifted the toilet lid and seat, pulled his prick through the fly of his jeans and sighed with relief as he let loose a stream of piss.

"You're fucking kidding me right now, right?" Charlie hissed. She stood in the doorway of the dark bathroom. "Are you serious?"

"Hey, don't look!" Evan said as he swiveled his hips so his back was to her. The sound of his stream died. He looked over his shoulder at her shadowy figure in the dark. "I can't go with you standing there."

"Don't worry, I'm going." She turned and stormed away.

"Hey, wait," Evan said as he zipped himself up. "You're not 'going' going are you?" He rushed out in the hallway after her, grabbing her shoulder before she reached the garage.

"Get off me," she said angrily brushing his hand away.

"Charlie, stop," he said as she grabbed the doorknob.

She turned and faced him but they could barely see each other in the dark house. It was their first burglary together and they had found a house in an affluent suburb on the east side of the city. It was almost seven o'clock at night and all the lights inside and outside of the home were off and there were a lot of shrubbery and trees surrounding the property that made it an ideal target hiding entry points from the street and neighbors.

They had parked Evan's car a half mile away in a Holiday Inn parking lot near the freeway. Before exiting the car they used Evan's smart phone to view their targeted house on a satellite image and picked out two different lines of escape from the house back to the hotel parking lot. They left their phones in the center console, locked Evan's Lexus and hid the key behind the driver side back tire. That way either of them could get into the vehicle in case they got split up. They casually walked back to the home as if they were a couple out for an evening stroll.

Evan had been excited yet disappointed to find a back door to the garage unlocked. He had really hoped to try out his new lock picking skill for the very first time in a real setting. A large part of him wanted to impress Charlie, to show her he could be her equal. He had been practicing his picking skills on half a dozen different locks he'd purchased at Home Depot and all but one of them he could easily open in less than a minute. The door from the garage to the house was also unlocked.

"No, you stop, Evan," Charlie said as they stood facing each other in the dark. "You shouldn't be doing this. You're not cut out for it."

"What are you talking about?"

"What's with you pissing? You did it in that first house and now you're doing it here. Is it some sort of perverted animal thing, like you've got to mark your territory or some shit like that?"

"No, I just really had to go," Evan said. "Maybe it's nerves or something."

"That's my point. You're not cut out for this."

"I am too."

"And you don't even need to be doing it. You've got money."

"Everyone can always use more."

"Yeah, well me working with you means less for me, doesn't it?" Charlie said. "I don't like having to split what I make."

"Fine. You can keep it all. It will be like an apprenticeship for me."

Charlie shook her head. "There's something seriously wrong with you, isn't there?"

Evan figured there was no good answer. "Can we just do this?" he asked. "We're wasting a lot of time just standing here."

He had a point. Charlie usually tried to be in and out of any house she burglarized within six minutes. She had come up with that time frame after reading an article online that pointed out that even if a house had an alarm, the average time it took the alarm company to even call the police was seven minutes. Once the alarm company was triggered the company's first task was to attempt to contact the homeowner, which consisted of two and sometimes three contact numbers: home, office and cellular. This was due to the fact that ninety-seven percent of triggered security systems were false alarms. If the homeowner couldn't be reached or verified that they weren't home, the security company called 911, which in turn would call the appropriate local authorities.

Even though Charlie was pretty certain this home didn't have an alarm, they'd still been in there longer than she'd liked. They should already be leaving but as it was they hadn't even started.

"Okay," Charlie said, "but you do exactly as I say. First of all, where are you gloves?"

"I took them off to pee."

"Well put them back on and then flush the toilet. You don't want to leave your DNA waiting in the toilet for when the cops arrive."

Evan did as she said and then followed her quickly through the house. She first went to the front and back doors, unlocking both, giving them a total of three avenues of escape. Then she went to the master bedroom and found a dark, oversized purse in the closet, which she utilized to put all of the homeowner's jewelry in that was found in the jewelry boxes - one on a bedroom dresser and the other in the bathroom - dresser drawers, and nightstands.

There was a mostly empty guest bedroom, a sewing room that they ignored except for checking the closet for any type of safe, and a small den where she found a desk drawer containing three Planter's Peanuts cans with old silver coins. Everything went into the purse, she locked the front and back doors as well as locked the garage door that led to the backyard so it wouldn't be obviously evident how they had gotten in.

They walked swiftly but casually back to their car in the hotel parking lot. They were both elated and giddy with adrenaline as they drove onto the freeway and back to Evan's apartment.

The next three burglaries over the following two weeks went off without a hitch. It wasn't until the blue two-story home where things went to shit.

"I don't like it," Evan said.

"It's perfect," Charlie countered as the Lexus drove casually past the target house. She pulled up a satellite view of the neighborhood on her phone. "There's a bowling alley and strip mall just three streets over. Take a left here."

"We should stay with single story homes," Evan said as he followed her directions. "There's always a chance you could get trapped on the top floor if the owners come home."

"That's ridiculous. Have you ever known any burglars caught on the second floor?"

"I've seen it in a movie or two."

Charlie shook her head. "When are you going to realize real life isn't like the movies?"

Twenty minutes later they were trapped in a closet on the second floor of the blue house.

"Ronald, hurry up," a woman's voice called out from the upstairs bedroom as Charlie and Evan approached the doorway. Evan bumped into Charlie as she spun around, both of their eyes wide with fright and surprise. Charlie pushed him back the other way they'd come from down the hall.

Before they reached the stairs a man's voice rose from the first floor: "You're not going to believe this!"

Evan spun around and Charlie bumped into him. "What do we do?" Evan hissed, so scared now he was sure he was about to piss his pants. He wished he had gone as soon as they'd gotten into the house.

"In here," Charlie whispered as she reached for the nearest door in the hallway. They stepped into a small laundry room with a washer, dryer, large sink and counter and an accordion closet door. She closed the door softly behind them as they heard the man climb the stairs.

"I got soaked," the man said, his voice growing louder and closer.

"See, I told you," Evan whispered in the dark room. There was a faint gray light coming from a small window.

"Shut up," Charlie whispered back as she stepped to the window between the dryer and the counter. She was angry that she'd found herself in this predicament. The house had looked empty but they hadn't tried ringing the doorbell or knocking first, a step she oftentimes took before entering a home. "We can jump out here," she whispered looking out the window at the shrubbery below.

Evan shook his head and whispered, "No way. I can't jump."

"We have to," Charlie hissed.

"We have to get you out of those clothes," the woman of the house said out in the hallway. "No, not in the bedroom, you're dripping. In the laundry room."

"Shit!" Charlie hissed. "There!" She pushed Evan toward the sliding accordion closet door. The closet was lined with shelves of linen and towels and there was a vacuum standing next to a broom in the corner. There was barely enough room for Charlie to close the door and it jammed on its track three inches from closing.

The laundry room light came on and a bar of light cut into the closet from the large slit in the door. Evan and Charlie stood facing the door, their bodies pressed against each other, Evan's front to Charlie's back, and they both tried to lean their bodies away from the light, but could still see into the laundry room.

"Marla, I swear, if I ever get my hands on that rinky dink contractor," the man in his mid-thirties said. He was about five-eight with blonde, curly hair that was dripping wet, as were the green, pinstripe pajama tops and bottoms he was wearing.

"It's not his fault, it's the plumber's," Marla replied. She was a couple inches shorter than the man and had dark auburn hair not quite shoulder length. She was a little plump and wearing an oversized pink nightshirt that hung to her knees. "Put them in here," she told Ronald as she opened the top of the washer.

Ronald pulled off the sopping wet pajama top and dropped it in the washer and then untied his bottoms and slid them off exposing his nakedness.

"The water must be cold," Marla said and Ronald glanced down at his shriveled member as he dropped his bottoms in the washer. "I'm kidding. I'll get you a towel," she said as she approached the closet.

Evan and Charlie tensed, their bodies preparing for fight or flight.

"There's one right here," Ronald said as he grabbed one off the countertop. As he dried himself he said, "The basement is ruined, the new rug, everything on the floor. I'm telling you, this whole house is one thing after another."

Marla put soap in the washing machine, shut the lid and started it up. "So we'll get rid of it," she said simply as she leaned against the washer and watched her husband bend over and finish drying himself.

"But we just finished renovating it. I thought you--"

"I'm kinda over it."

"Really?" Ronald asked as he approached her and the washer. He popped open the lid and tossed the towel in with his pajamas. "It has been one problem after another, hasn't it?"

"But we've had our fun here," Marla said. She glanced at Ronald's crotch. "Not so cold anymore?"

"I guess I'm a little excited at the prospect of selling this place."

"Is that all?"

Ronald shook his head. "I was thinking of the first time we christened this room."

Marla smiled and looked at the washing machine. "It's another five minutes until the spin cycle begins."

"Wanna go for a ride?"

Ronald's hard cock was long and slender and poking out of his blonde tangle of pubes. He helped pull the nightshirt over Marla's head. She had breasts that hung down like half footballs with dark tipped nipples. She was wearing a pair of blue panties that had two cartoon bunnies on the front. She pulled them off exposing a dark tangle of fur and then Ronald put his hands under her armpits and helped her up onto the washer.

Charlie felt Evan's boner poking into her backside.

"You gotta lick it before you stick it," Marla said as she spread her legs apart on the washer. Ronald bent forward and nuzzled his face between her legs. "UH-huh, that's it. You do mommy right." She grabbed his wet hair in both her hands and pulled him into her crotch. "Uh! Uh! Uh! Get it!" she grunted.

Evan's boner was sliding side to side, rubbing against Charlie's ass. She didn't know what he was doing behind her but she didn't like it. She jerked her hips backwards into him.

"Umph!" Evan gasped and then bit down on Charlie's shoulder to keep from crying out in pain. Charlie gritted her teeth and elbowed Evan in the ribs.

"Would you stop hitting me!" Evan hissed in her ear.

"Stop poking me," she whispered back.

"I can't help it."

Five feet away Ronald had stood up and was poking his wife, his cock rocking back and forth in her as her body vibrated atop the washing machine on its spin cycle. Marla's tits jiggled like water balloons in an earthquake and she began crying out like a wounded yodeler as earthquakes of her own rumbled through her body. Ronald's skinny white ass was jerking wildly, his hands clasped to his wife's thick thighs and then he was screaming out, "Oh mommy! Oh mommy!" as he spurt his juices into her.

The washing machine was still rumbling and spinning as Ronald helped his wife down and they left the laundry room talking about where they might move to and when they could get the plumber to come out.

"Have you ever seen such a white ass?" Charlie said after they were safely back to the car.

"I wasn't really looking at his ass," Evan replied as he drove them out of the neighborhood.

"Then how did you know I was talking about him?"

"I mean I saw it, but I was looking more at her."

"You couldn't see one without the other. Obviously something had you turned on. You're going to have to put your pants and shorts in the wash when you get home."

"Why are you giving me such a hard time? You were watching it, too."

"You were the one trying to give the hard time. And me watching it is different because I'm not a pervert like you."

"Whatever," Evan said. "You liked it, too. Your nipples were almost poking through your shirt."

"What were you doing looking at my nipples, perv? And that was just because I was scared."

"Uh-huh, and so was my boner. It was scared and looking for a place to hide."

# CHAPTER 11

Evan and Charlie were looking for a place to hide. Charlie couldn't believe they'd been caught inside a house once again by a homeowner. After this, she was done, she told herself. Either she was losing her touch or having Evan with was bad luck; either way she needed to step away for a while, time to go someplace new.

They had taken a couple weeks off after their last close call and being trapped in the laundry room closet. During that time Evan had been canvassing the neighborhoods and he had found a nice single story suburban home that he said would be perfect.

"They're obviously on vacation," Evan said, "because they haven't put their trash cans out for the past two weeks."

"That's no guarantee. I knew of someone who used to take their trash to a Dumpster so they didn't have to pay for waste management."

"Give me a break. Someone with a three hundred thousand dollar home isn't skimping to save twenty dollars a month."

"You don't know," Charlie argued, "a lot of millionaires are misers."

"You can't give up and be scared just because of a little mishap last time."

"I'm not scared. And it wasn't a little mishap. We were that close," she spread her thumb and forefinger an inch apart, "from being caught."

"But we weren't, we got away. And I promise you this house is empty."

And it was.

"See, I told you the lights were on timers," Evan said as he pointed out the boxes plugged into the outlets. He was excited and feeling good, especially after being able to pick the lock to the back door to get them inside. It might have taken him a couple minutes longer than it would have Charlie, but he'd pulled it off and he could tell Charlie was impressed, even if she didn't say anything.

"Let's just make it quick, okay?" Charlie said as they rushed towards the master bedroom. But they weren't quick enough.

"That was quick," Detective Fox said as Nanae got into his car.

"I told you I already had it," she said as she showed him the baggie of meth.

He snatched it from her hand. "How'd you get it?"

"I got my ways," she said with a sly smile.

"That you do," Fox said and squeezed her bony thigh, the edge of his palm rubbing against her crotch.

"We going to Regent?"

"Yeah. You get that fixed down there?" he asked, his hand pushing against her pussy.

She shook her head. "I gotta have surgery."

"You got cysts in your ass?"

"What?"

"Don't worry, we'll figure something out."

Fox's phone vibrated and as soon as he looked at it he hit the brakes on his car and slid to a stop at the curb.

"Get out," Fox told Nanae.

"What?" she said looking confused and hurt.

He reached across her and opened the door. "Get the fuck out!" He shoved her out onto her ass as she made a comment about smoking up but he was already burning rubber as the car bolted down the street. He swung a hard right at the corner and the passenger door slammed shut.

Fox's heart raced as he gunned the engine and blasted through stop signs while at the same time pulling his gun from his holster and shoving it under his thigh, ready for quick action. The little baggie of meth he shoved into his pants pocket.

"It looks like meth," Charlie said. "Leave it."

"Have you ever done it?" Evan asked as he set the baggie back on the night stand next to the king sized bed. "It's worth money, isn't it? We could sell it."

"You get caught with that and you're looking at serious time. And to sell it you have to deal with junkies and it's not worth the hassle."

Charlie was going through the dresser drawers, always starting with the bottom one first so she didn't have to waste precious seconds closing them as she moved to the next one.

"You didn't say if you tried it," Evan said as he opened the nightstand drawer.

"I've tried a lot of things. So what?"

"I was just asking. Hey, look at this," he said and pulled two fancy watches out of the drawer. "One of them has diamonds all over the face."

"Probably fake. Put it in the bag. Go faster."

Evan dropped it into the small backpack he was holding in his left hand. He looked over at Charlie who was rummaging through the closet. "Finding anything good?"

"Obviously just a guy's place. All men's clothes. No jewelry boxes. Not finding anything in the suit pockets."

"Holy shit, look at this!"

Charlie peeked out of the closet to see Evan holding an AK-47. "Put that down!" she yelled.

Her scream scared him and if he'd had his finger on the trigger he'd surely have shot off a round.

"What's your deal?" Evan asked. "It's got to be worth some good money."

Charlie stomped over to him, looking and acting like an irate parent. "I told you we don't mess with guns or drugs. That's my rule and you agreed you'd play by my rules."

"I know but--"

"Put it back. Now!"

Evan slipped it back under the bed where he'd found it and then followed Charlie out of the bedroom. It seemed like this house he'd thought looked so good was going to turn out to be a bust. There was nice furniture and electronics and paintings, but no cash and not much jewelry, the only two things Charlie was interested in.

"We'll check out down here real quick and then we're out of here," Charlie said as she and Evan walked downstairs to the basement.

"Holy shit!" Evan exclaimed as Charlie shined her small flashlight around.

Then they heard someone upstairs.

Fox had parked his car a house away, not wanting to spook the intruders in his own home. His phone had been sent the first alert when the motion sensors in the back yard had been tripped. When the back door of the home had been breached, a second alert was sent to his phone. He wasn't surprised to find the front door unlocked - whoever was inside was obviously a professional and making sure they had more than one escape. Fox hadn't seen a lookout in any vehicle as he ran to his house, but if they were good they'd have someone hiding in the bushes or shadows across the street and signaling them to get out.

As he was about to push open the front door he received a phone alert informing him the basement motion sensors had been triggered. That pissed him off but also excited him because there was only one way out of the basement and that was back up the stairs. It also meant they were still here. He turned off his phone so it wouldn't give away his position with any more alerts and then Fox bolted into his house, his gun at the ready and looking for targets as he made his way to the top of the basement stairs.

Fox kept his back pressed against the wall next to the doorway to the basement but had his gun pointed down the hallway to his master bedroom. His heart was thumping heavy in his chest and the adrenaline raged through his veins. He wished he would have grabbed the ballistic vest out of the trunk of his car. But then he remembered the AK that had been under his bed that he kept meaning to put into one of his safes; if the intruder had that his vest would be useless anyways.

Fox took a deep breath and held it, listening for any and all sounds in the house. Everything was quiet except for the blood he could hear throbbing in his ears. He moved cautiously to the bedroom door at the end of the hall, his head jerking back and forth from the bedroom to the basement door. He needed to know if anyone was in the bedroom and more importantly if they had his assault rifle because that could change everything.

"I wish we had that AK," Evan whispered in the dark. He was hiding behind a six-foot tall gun safe at the far end of the basement.

Charlie was hiding behind a similar gun safe six feet away. There were a total of six large gun safes on the cold, concrete floor and in one corner a washer and dryer. Nothing else was in the basement, including no windows or doors. The only way out was back up the stairway they had come down.

"You really think you could kill somebody?" Charlie whispered back. It was too dark for them to even see each other after Charlie had turned off her mini flashlight.

"No, I wouldn't shoot them. Just point it at them."

"You don't point a gun unless you're willing to use it."

"Well, I mean if I had to--"

"Shh! They're moving around upstairs."

"Maybe they won't even know we're here," Evan whispered, getting his hopes up. "We could sneak out after they go to sleep or something."

"Would you be quiet!" Charlie hissed.

There was the sound of more movement upstairs, the floor creaking above them. Charlie had a very bad feeling about this. Yep, she was definitely done going into houses for a while, maybe for good.

The basement light came on, blinding both of them briefly. They looked at each other crouched behind their respective safes. Yet they felt anything but safe.

A voice boomed through the hollow basement, echoing off the cement walls. "Sheriff's Department! I know you're down here. Come out with your hands up! If you have anything in your hands you will be shot. Come out now!"

Charlie set her backpack on the floor, about to come out from behind the safe but then saw Evan waving at her to stay put. She crinkled her brow and gave him a confused look.

"This is your last chance!" the voice boomed.

Evan held his hand in a stop gesture to Charlie and then he stood up and called out as he stepped from behind his safe. "Don't shoot. It's just me. I'm unarmed."

"Show me your hands!" the voice screamed at him, which Evan thought was ridiculous because his hands were up. At the other end of the basement where the stairs were Evan could see a partial head and an extended arm holding a gun pointed at him.

"Turn around! Now walk backwards to me. Interlace your fingers behind your head. Keep coming backwards." Evan did as he was told. "Stop! Get on your knees. Don't you fucking move!"

Evan heard swift movement behind him and then a handcuff was slammed hard around his left wrist and his arm was jerked behind him at the same time his other wrist was yanked violently from his head and cuffed behind his back. A foot kicked him hard in the middle of his back knocking him to the concrete floor which he hit with the side of his face and bit his tongue.

"Who else is with you," the man demanded.

The wind had been knocked out of him and he was struggling to breathe as Evan said, "It's just me. Really."

"If you fucking move I'll kill you," the man growled and began moving into the basement with his gun leading the way.

Evan knew he had to distract him, couldn't let him find Charlie. "Hey!" Evan cried out. "Hey, asshole. I told you I'm the only--"

Charlie screamed at the same time the man yelled, "Show me your hands! Get out here!" And then her body was flying face first in the middle of the basement. She caught herself with her hands and then the man was on her back yelling, "Put your arms out! Don't you fucking move!"

The man's left hand moved up and down her body as he held his gun in his right hand. She flinched when his rough touching hit her thigh wound but not when his hand cupped her crotch or felt up both her tits; she expected it. She only assumed it would get worse, especially once she was booked into county jail and would have to strip naked and squat and cough. It wouldn't be her first time.

"This obviously isn't your first time," Fox said as he stood looking at the two young burglars in front of him. They both had their hands cuffed behind them and he had seated them on his cushy living room couch. "But you're obviously not professionals either."

Evan's tongue was swollen in his mouth where he'd bit it. He tried pleading with the stocky man standing in front of them with his arms crossed. "Sir, we don't--"

"Don't sir me," Fox growled. "And don't you fucking lie to me. Did Cole send you?"

"We don't know a Cole," Evan said shaking his head. "This was all an accident."

The man's beefy paw shot out and backhanded Evan, snapping his head back and bringing tears to his eyes. "You didn't accidentally leave your house after dark wearing dark clothes and carrying lock picks. Lie to me again and I'll hurt you."

Evan was thinking that hit was quite painful and certainly didn't want to see what any further pain would entail. He didn't like the guy in front of them and he wondered if he was really a cop or not. He also wondered which would be scarier, if he was or wasn't a cop.

"How about you, sweet thing," Fox said turning his attention to Charlie. "You haven't said a word. Do you and your little boyfriend here do this a lot?"

Charlie nodded her head. She didn't like the way this guy would look at her, his gaze on her tits rather than her eyes. It was something she was pretty used to dealing with, but not while handcuffed in some guy's living room. She wondered if the man was questioning them until uniformed police officers arrived to take them to jail.

"What made you pick my house?" Fox asked.

"You don't put out your garbage cans," Evan said.

"I'm talking to her, not you," Fox said. Evan flinched from his words, afraid they may be followed by a hand. Fox considered the information and internally kicked himself for his carelessness. He didn't live at this stash house, it wasn't in his name, and none of his crew knew about the place. It's where he kept all the extra that he skimmed from the jobs as well as some of his side projects. It was important that the home kept up appearances in the neighborhood so no one would ever look twice at it. It was also for this reason there was no way he was going to arrest these two intruders and have to explain the house and make reports. No, he had something else in mind for this boy and girl.

Fox spent the next forty minutes questioning them and typing their personal information into his computer. He went to his basement and returned with a crime kit and proceeded to take their fingerprints and DNA swabs and then finished by taking front and side photos of both of them.

"You two are not to leave the city," Fox told them. "I'm going to call you within the next week and you're going to answer and do what you're told. Understand?"

Evan and Charlie nodded their heads.

"If you try to run or duck me, I'll have you plastered on news stations looking worse than satanic baby killers. Who knows where they'll find your DNA or prints."

He uncuffed them and told them to get out of his house. Charlie and Evan looked at each other in shock.

# CHAPTER 12

Marco was pretty certain that Ophelia was in shock. She'd barely said a word their entire flight home, sleeping most of the way, and once he'd gotten her to the town home she'd gone straight to bed and now sixteen hours later she was still there. He wasn't even sure if she'd gotten up to use the bathroom.

He sat on the edge of the bed next to her covered form. She was lying on her side facing him in the darkened room, the light from the hallway barely enough to illuminate them. He placed his hand atop her hip and rubbed it gently through the covers. Ophelia opened her eyes and gave him a half smile.

"How are you doing?" he asked her softly.

She shrugged her shoulders.

"Can I get you something to eat?" he asked.

She shook her head.

"You've got to eat, baby. I could bring it to you in bed."

She shrugged her shoulders.

"What can I get you?"

She mumbled something and Marco bent closer to her and asked her to repeat it.

"I want to go see my mom," Ophelia said, her voice soft and childlike.

"Okay, fine," Marco answered soothingly. "I'll take you to see her. Where is she?"

Ophelia mumbled.

"I can't hear you, baby."

"Tehran."

It was a sixteen-hour flight with a layover at Heathrow, and after Marco had booked their first class tickets Ophelia had become a little more herself, but he could still tell she was subdued. He was patient and understanding with her, even if he didn't fully grasp how or why she could be so upset and emotional over what she had seen, the death of someone she didn't even know. Maybe if it had been a priest that she'd actually gone to church with, Marco could at least see her being a little distraught, but he was a complete stranger.

Every single day more than a hundred and fifty thousand people died in thousands of different ways: heart attacks, cancer, disease, drowning, falls, fires, car, plane, and motorcycle accidents, wars, famine, shootings, stabbings, strangulations, freak accidents, calculated suicides, paid assassinations, floods, earthquakes, volcanoes, tornadoes, hurricanes, viruses, plagues, heat, cold. The world was a violent, dangerous place and it was more astonishing to Marco that as many people stayed alive as they did.

And for those that he helped to an earlier demise, he didn't see how it made much difference in the grand scheme of things. Once a job was done, it was done and he had never given it a second thought, didn't think about the target's family or friends or the impact the person's death would have. Even when he'd done political assassinations for shadow governments, he didn't contemplate what difference the death might make in regards to entire nations of people.

That wasn't his job, that's not what he was paid for. Others had made those decisions and calculations and they hired him to make it happen; if he wasn't available they'd simply hire someone else. The world was full of killers, most in uniformed military and police occupations, but also plenty in the private sector.

Marco wanted to empathize with Ophelia, truly wanted to understand her so he could do all in his power to see that she was never hurt or feeling like this again. Before this incident he'd contemplated what it would be like if he told her the truth about what he did, but now he knew that was never an option. She could never know what he did.

"I know you did that," Ophelia said to him as the plane soared thirty-five thousand feet over the Atlantic Ocean.

"What did I do?" Marco asked as he held the hand of his beautiful lady in the seat beside him.

"You told that little girl to bring her giraffe for me to hug."

"I swear to you I didn't. But it was cute."

When they were at the airport waiting to board the plane, a small black girl with purple ribbons in her hair walked up to Ophelia with a two foot tall stuffed giraffe outstretched in her hands.

"Do you want to hug her?" the six-year-old asked Ophelia.

With tears in her eyes Ophelia hugged the stuffed toy and handed it back to the girl and told her thank you. Marco had been returning from a magazine stand when he saw it all take place.

"I'm doing better," Ophelia said now almost seven hours into the flight.

Marco squeezed her hand. "Good. I've been worried about you."

Ophelia smiled and laid her head on his shoulder.

"You know," Marco said, "we're almost five miles up in the sky. If you thought the two mile high club was exciting...."

"I don't think I can right now," Ophelia said and gave his hand a squeeze. "I'm sorry."

"You don't need to apologize. We have all the time in the world. I'm not going anywhere."

Ophelia began to cry and he held her tightly.

A cute, blond stewardess in a blue and white uniform and the name tag Chandra over her perky little breasts approached and put her hand on Marco's shoulder. "Can I get you anything?"

"Do you want anything, honey?" Marco asked Ophelia. She kept her eyes shut and shook her head against his chest. "We're okay for now," he said to Chandra.

The stewardess squeezed his shoulder and gave him a wink. "If you need anything at all, don't hesitate to ask. I'll check back on you in a little while," she said and walked away, her slender hips and tight little ass swaying beneath her blue skirt. She glanced over her shoulder and smiled at Marco watching her.

Marco closed his eyes and pondered what she meant by that. He was used to women flirting and being attracted to him but since he'd been with Ophelia he didn't give a second thought to wondering what it would be like to fuck other women. There had been nothing sexually Ophelia wouldn't do, but it was even more than that, something almost beyond comprehension that he felt with her, like she was as vital to him as air and food. And when she hurt, he hurt, even if he didn't fully understand why.

When Marco awoke the plane was dark, everything in gray shadows. The seat beside him was empty and outside the plane window far below he could see tiny white-capped waves shimmering in the moonlight. He stood up and walked down the aisle looking for Ophelia, everyone was in their seats slumped over asleep. He spotted Chandra at the stewardess station in front of first class.

"I thought you were going to check back on me?" he asked her.

Chandra smiled and pressed up against him. He could feel her excited stiff nipples against his chest through the fabric of her white blouse. "The five mile high club is five times more fun than the mile high club," she said as the pushed her hand into the front of his pants and grabbed his cock.

"Shouldn't we go to the restroom?" Marco asked.

"No one will wake up," she said as she pulled his dick out of his pants. She bent over at the waist and wrapped her lips around the head of his shaft. Marco leaned forward and pulled her skirt up over her hips baring her small, white ass that was like two perfect half moons. He rubbed the velvety warm flesh of her ass as she sucked him, sliding her mouth up and down the length of his stiff cock.

Just as he was getting into it and moving his hips in sync with her mouth, she stood and pressed her body into his again. Her shirt was open and his was off and her perky nipples tickled his chest. She put her mouth next to his ear, her breath hot against his skin. "I want you to stick me."

His hand slid from cupping her ass to the underside of her thigh and he lifted her leg. They were both naked from the waist down and he saw she wasn't a true blonde, the small triangle above her pussy a dark arrow pointing down. He slipped his cock into her warm, wet slit beneath the triangle, his hand squeezing her thigh and opening her up.

"Oh fuck! Stick me harder!" Chandra cried as she clung to his shoulders, her fingernails digging into his back.

"Not so loud," Marco said as he thrust into her over and over, his cock pounding against her pussy. "We don't want anyone to know."

"They're not waking up, Marco, never again," she said but the way she said his name was how Ophelia said it, with her sexy Persian accent. And then it was Ophelia's tits rubbing against his chest as he fucked her while standing up, Ophelia's ass in his hands.

Marco didn't look at her but instead his attention was on the plane full of sleeping passengers. But they weren't sleeping, they were dead. Some of them strangled, some shot, some blown up, some poisoned, every one of them a man, woman or child he had killed. The dark plane was full.

"Don't stop!" Ophelia cried out as she bounced on his cock.

"I have to," he said, though he didn't stop sticking her. "I have to stop."

"No!" she cried as orgasms ripped through her body and blood poured down her thighs. "No!"

Marco awoke to Ophelia crying out beside him. "It's okay, baby, I'm right here. Shh, it's okay." He held her as she shook in his arms. Chandra approached and Marco asked her for a couple of waters, not watching her ass this time when she walked away.

Ophelia's mother was almost seventy, but still vibrant and beautiful and insisted Marco call her O-mom. He also met her grandmother, ninety-one, whom everyone called Gramma Gigi. There was no mistaking that the three were related and Marco knew he'd be a lucky man if he was still with Ophelia when they were in their seventies because she'd be just as beautiful as she was today.

"Ophelia, go get your photo albums," her mother told her as they all sat in the modest living room.

"You can't be serious," Ophelia replied. "He doesn't want to see them."

"I'd love to," Marco said with a wide smile.

"I'm sure there's nothing in them he hasn't seen," Gramma Gigi said.

"Gramma Gigi!" Ophelia said blushing.

"Don't mind her," O-mom said. "Go get them."

Ophelia left the living room down a hallway lined with family photos on the walls. O-mom put her hand on Marco's knee and said, "My daughter is very happy with you. Thank you."

"I would like your blessing to make her even happier," Marco said.

O-mom beamed. "Does that mean what I think it means?"

"No more free milk," Gramma Gigi said.

"Huh?" Marco said.

"Never mind her," O-mom said. "Where do you want to have your wedding?"

"Wherever she wants," Marco replied. "I have an appointment with a ring designer when we return."

"We weren't a part of the last wedding, they didn't even have a reception," Ophelia's mother said. "If we did it here more of her family and relatives could afford to come."

"Money's no object," Marco said. "If she wants to have her wedding on the moon, I will make sure anyone who wants to go will be there."

"What conspiracies are you all talking about?" Ophelia asked as she returned to the living room with three large photo albums.

"We're talking about the moon," Gramma Gigi said.

Marco and Ophelia returned to their hotel in downtown Tehran after only a few hours at her mother's home. The jet lag and time difference was taking its toll and Ophelia wanted to rest up for tomorrow when they planned to spend the day with many of her aunts, uncles and cousins, a little get together her mother had excitedly arranged.

"Gramma Gigi has a lot of spunk," Marco said.

"I don't know why she insists on pointing out every naked picture of me in the photo albums."

Marco laughed. "I think the real question is why there are so many naked pictures of you."

"I went through an anti-clothes phase, as you saw."

"I'm all for you going through that phase again any time," Marco told her.

Ophelia smiled and gave Marco a hug and kiss. "Will you unzip me, please? I want to take a bath before we lie down."

She turned her back to Marco and he pulled the zipper down from the back of her neck to her waist.

"What did your grandma mean by no more milk when I told them I was going to marry you?"

"Oh god, she didn't," Ophelia said as she walked to the bathroom while removing her dress. Marco heard the water in the tub begin to splash. Ophelia stepped out of the bathroom in white lace panties and bra. "She would tell me that no man buys the cow if he can get the milk for free."

Marco looked her body up and down and then approached her and took her in his arms. "You are far from a cow." He kissed her neck and shoulder while reaching behind her and undoing her bra. She slipped her arms out of it and Marco tossed the bra on the bed and cupped one of her breasts gently in his hand, his thumb grazing her nipple.

"Can we do this after we rest?" Ophelia asked softly.

"Of course we can," Marco said. He kissed the top of her breast he held in his hand before she turned away to the bathroom.

"Is there any sparkling water?" she asked as she turned off the water taps.

Marco went to the mini fridge and found a Perrier. He loosened the top as he walked into the bathroom and then almost dropped the bottle when he looked up. In the bathtub was the dead, bloated, wrinkly body of Abigail Orr floating on her back. Marco blinked and then it was Ophelia looking at him worriedly.

"Marco, are you okay?

"Just jet lag," he told her and brought her the water.

In the morning Marco answered the door, having been waiting for the knock from room service.

"May I come in?" the young man in the hotel uniform asked. The young man's face was blue and around his neck was an industrial strength zip tie cinched so tight there were rivulets of blood dripping onto his white collar. Marco had killed him two and a half years ago in Montana.

"Sir? Your breakfast?"

No, it was just the hotel wait staff and Marco let him into the room.

After breakfast Marco and Ophelia sat on the small hotel balcony outside their bedroom, both in hotel robes, looking out over the city.

"You're so quiet this morning," Ophelia said.

"I didn't sleep well," Marco told her truthfully. Every time he closed his eyes he saw the faces of those he had killed. Hundreds of faces.

"Is it me?" Ophelia asked. "Because I didn't want--"

He put his hand on her knee. "It's not you at all."

Ophelia pulled the fabric of her robe off her leg so Marco's hand was on her flesh. "We have a little time before we have to leave," she told him.

He squeezed her leg and looked deep into her eyes before saying, "Let's take our time."

# CHAPTER 13

"Nothing like taking your sweet ass time," Detective Fox said.

"Not me," Detective Hansel said. "You tell me one dealer you know that can keep an appointment on time." He had just walked into the back room of Rusty's where the other four cops were playing cards at the poker table.

"I've known a few criminals," Winters said, "that would make great company executives if they gave two shits and actually applied themselves."

Sergeant took a drink of his Maker's Mark and then said, "They'd rather get high and fuck people over."

"Yeah," Winters said, "but so do many CEO's. The difference is the CEO's put forth the effort and time to go to work every day."

"And drug dealers don't?" Hansel asked.

Cole shook his head. "It's not about applying themselves. It's about who grew up with opportunity of schooling and a decent home with supportive parents, as most who become CEO's did. Whereas most of your dealers and criminals were dealt a bad hand with fucked up families and early drug use and dropping out of school."

"That's bullshit," Fox said. "Most criminals are simply pieces of shit looking for a shortcut to the good life without having to put in the years of work."

Hansel placed four envelopes on the table in front of him. "And what are we doing?" he asked as he tossed each of the men an envelope.

"We're risking our lives," Sergeant said, "keeping our city safe to get paid what, sixty or seventy grand a year? Some of these pukes we deal with make that in an hour. And with that kind of money they have the best in firepower and don't hesitate to use it on us. If there's anyone who deserves extra hazard pay, it's us."

"Here, here," said Winters raising his glass.

"Twenty-two hundred, that's it?" Fox said as he thumbed through the bills in the envelope.

"Don't start," Sergeant said, giving him a look.

Fox raised his hands. "What? I was just asking a question."

"Yeah, that's it," Hansel said.

"Price of drugs must be going down," Fox mumbled and stuffed the envelope into his pocket.

"Actually," Winters said, "prices around here are starting to rise. I think Casablanca will be making his move within the next ten days."

"Do we have enough to move on him?" Sergeant asked.

"It's hard to tell what's coming or going at either the auto shop or plumbing company because both have garages. We've got no one inside."

"Can we get to anyone close to him?" Sergeant asked. "Or what about one of his girls? Can we play them against each other?"

"There's nothing like a woman scorned," Hansel said.

"The girls know about each other," Fox said. "They even do a little three-way action and orgies."

"How the fuck do you find out something like that?" Winters asked.

"I make it a point to get into my work," Fox said with a smile.

"Do we have pictures of these ladies? I want to see them," Winters said.

"They're hot," Cole replied. "We've got photos of them in and out of the houses."

"Not of the threesomes?" Winters asked.

"Can we get back on track here," Sergeant said. "We've got ten days to make something happen."

"Within a week I'm going to call you and you're going to burgle a house," Fox said. He was sitting in a Burger King booth with a half eaten Whopper in front of him. Across from him was Evan and Charlie, neither of them in the mood to eat anything.

Charlie shook her head. "This is crazy. You say you're a cop yet you want us to commit crimes. How do we even know you're really a cop? I never saw a badge."

Fox pulled out his gold detective shield and slapped it on the table. Both Charlie and Evan stared at it and the words that read Sacramento Sheriff's Department. "Anyone can buy a badge online," Charlie said.

Fox had taken a bite of his burger and was getting tired of screwing around. "Listen you little shit," he said to Charlie, a glob of chewed food rolling around in his mouth, "you'll do exactly as I say or you can spend the next five to fifteen in lock up."

"But you didn't even make a police report," Evan said. "There's no proof of anything."

Fox swallowed his burger and raised his eyebrows. "Proof? Evan Gabriel Hunt, age twenty-five, born and raised in Sacramento, parents married thirty-one years. How about your fingerprints in at least six burglaries, is that proof enough?"

Charlie looked at Evan with an I-fucking-told-you-so look. Charlie turned back to Fox and said, "My fingerprints aren't at any crime scenes."

"No, they're not. Charlie Candice Bonner, age nineteen, arrested for solicitation last year in Phoenix, no permanent address, mother in Iowa, father in federal prison for another seven years. That little bruise on your thigh must have come from the fence where there's some blood that matches your DNA. There was quite a bit of blood there, you're lucky you didn't die."

Evan felt a sense of pride that he'd had the skill to save her life. Of course that didn't seem to make up for the fact that Charlie kept blaming him at least a dozen times in the past two days that she was done with burglary, and now here they were being forced into doing it. Evan didn't mind so much because he still wanted to do burglaries, but he was also smart enough to see the bind they were in.

"What do we get out of this deal?" Evan asked.

Fox laughed. "Are you kidding? You get to not go to jail and not get that cute mouth of yours used as a cockpit."

"We want a cut," Charlie said. "And a guarantee."

"How about I guarantee that if you don't help me your DNA will miraculously show up at the next crime scene."

"You're going to plant my DNA and pin a crime on me that I didn't do?" Charlie asked.

Fox came out of the booth, his arm shooting across the table and knocking over his large Coke. He gripped the front of Charlie's green hoodie and yanked her towards him. "Let me see your hands!" Fox growled, his hamburger breath in her face.

Evan cringed against the wall, both in fear of Fox and to avoid the Coke dripping off the edge of the table.

"Show me your fucking hands!" Fox said, his eyes drilling into Charlie's.

A mother picked up her young son's food two tables away and pulled him quickly out of the restaurant.

Charlie raised her left hand from out of her lap.

"Both of them," Fox demanded.

Slowly Charlie's right hand rose above the table.

"L-let her go," Evan said. He wasn't sure if the cop was hurting Charlie or scaring her, but she looked about ready to cry.

"Shut your mouth," Fox told Evan without taking his eyes off Charlie. "You move and I'll smash you. Now Charlie, place your hands on the tabletop. Do it now."

Charlie set her hands on the table, one of them in a puddle of Coke.

"Don't fucking move," Fox said as he slid out of his booth, still holding Charlie with his right hand. His left hand plunged between Charlie's legs.

"Hey!" Evan said.

Fox's hand pushed against Charlie's crotch and then slid under her ass. She remained perfectly still, her only movement the blinking away of tears.

"You think you're pretty fucking cute, don't you?" Fox said as he pulled his left hand from between her legs. He was holding her phone that was playing a tape recording app.

Fox sat back in his booth and looked at Evan. "Where's your phone?"

"I don't have it with."

"Don't lie to me."

"I'm not."

Fox removed the battery from Charlie's phone and then snapped her phone in half like it was a graham cracker. Charlie took her hands off the table and sat back in the booth.

"Either of you try any shit like that again and it won't be an inanimate object that gets broken. Make no mistake, I'm in charge here and I've got you by the balls." Fox looked at Evan and then to Charlie. "Or in your case, the cunt hairs."

Evan subconsciously glanced down at Charlie's crotch and wondered if she had cunt hairs or if she was clean-shaven. He remembered her sleeping on his couch and her underwear riding up into her crotch, but it didn't register with him if she had any pubic hair or not. He felt himself getting a little chub in the Burger King booth and he quickly looked away from Charlie with the realization that she was right, he was a pervert.

Fox was still talking. "Get whatever tools together that you need and be ready to go when I call."

"A little hard to do when you busted my phone," Charlie said.

"I've got Evan's number," Fox said and began to slide out of the booth to go.

"We're going to need some money," Charlie said.

Fox stopped, not believing his ears. "What?"

"For supplies," Charlie said. "And I need a new phone."

Fox shook his head. "You try to set me up for blackmail using your phone and you think I'm going to give you money for another one? Are you on drugs?"

"How do we know what tools we'll need?" Evan asked, not because he cared about the answer but to try to draw the heat off of Charlie. "You haven't told us what we'll be burglarizing."

"Upper class home in a quiet neighborhood," Fox said. "Just like you've been doing. As for your supplies, use the money from all of your other jobs."

"There is none," Charlie lied. "Evan's a bad gambler. It's all gone."

Fox got out of the booth and Evan couldn't believe it when he saw him pull out a wad of folded bills from his pocket. He put two hundreds on the table in the spilled Coke. "If that's not enough then steal what you need."

After Fox left, Charlie picked up the wet bills and gave one to Evan.

"What the hell was that about?" Evan asked. "Were you trying to piss him off?"

"I was just trying to kind of see where his boundaries and limitations were."

"I thought he was going to hurt you," Evan said, "or... something else."

Charlie looked at him. "Thanks for sticking up for me."

Evan blushed. "I didn't do anything."

"You spoke up. That was enough. It's all you could do for now."

"What do you mean for now?"

"He's a dirty cop, we can't trust anything he tells us. We need to find a way to protect ourselves."

Evan glanced down at her crotch. "I didn't even realize you were recording him or trying to get him to say something."

Charlie nodded. "He's smart. But I've dealt with dirty cops before."

"Really?"

"Let's get out of here," Charlie said and slid out of the booth.

Evan followed and said, "I have to use the bathroom."

"Have you ever had your prostate checked?" Charlie asked. "Or your bladder? You piss more than an excited puppy."

As they drove back to Evan's he asked her, "So you've been to jail before?"

"Just for two nights," Charlie replied.

"For solicitation?"

"That's what they said."

"Is that... prostitution?"

"That's what they say."

"In Phoenix?"

"Yep."

"Did you like it in Phoenix?"

"Nope."

"Because of the dirty cops?"

"Can we stop with the interrogation," Charlie said.

Evan wondered what sort of ordeals she had been through and what she might have had to do in dealing with dirty cops. And he wondered how they were going to deal with the dirty cop that was now using them. I mean, come on, Evan thought, how do you beat a cop?

# CHAPTER 14

Marco was beating the cop with a heavy chain but the big Irish guy kept getting back up to his knees. His Boston police uniform was tattered and bloody and the man's scalp was cracked and bleeding. Marco had been told specifically no guns or knives were to be used on this hit, and a select few knew Marco was the one to call for specialty jobs like this one he performed eight years ago. It was a hefty payday, but the cop was making him earn his money.

Marco tackled the guy and wrapped the chain around his neck and began to squeeze the life out of him. But something was wrong. This wasn't how he'd done it.

The cop screamed his name. "Marco!" The cop didn't know his name and there was no way he could identify him with the ski mask he was wearing. Marco pulled tighter on the chain.

"Marco!" The cop's voice was high like a woman's. A woman with an accent.

Marco jerked awake in the king sized bed. Ophelia was gasping for breath beside him, a sheet wrapped around her neck, her eyes filled with terror and tears. Marco quickly loosened the sheet and pulled it away from Ophelia who bent over in bed and began coughing. Marco's hands shook as he backed away from her, not believing that he had been strangling her.

Ophelia had a hand to her throat and looked at Marco. The terror and shame in his eyes scared her. "It's okay, Marco. You were just having a nightmare."

Marco shook his head. It wasn't okay. He turned and went into the bathroom, closing the door behind him. He turned on the light and stared at himself in the mirror. What the fuck was going on? He'd never had any qualms with his job and what he did, never before been haunted by the faces of his victims, wasn't prone to nightmares.

Yet he'd also never before dealt with the residuals of his actions. Once he was done with a hit, he was done. He didn't look back, didn't look for accounts of what he did in the newspaper or online. To him, his job had as much significance as a mechanic performing an oil change; once the mechanic was finished, he moved onto the next vehicle without a second thought to how the previous car had fared with its new oil. He didn't care.

Now all of sudden Marco did care. Not about his victims but about how his victim had impacted Ophelia. They had returned from Tehran yesterday and though he'd managed to keep up a cheerful facade in front of her mother and grandmother, Ophelia knew something was wrong and was sure it was her fault. They had made love their last night at the hotel, slow and passionate, but it was missing the spark that was always so evident in their previous couplings. It was like drinking the open can of Pepsi left in the refrigerator overnight, still sweet but flat.

Marco had slept, or pretended to sleep, for most of the plane ride home. Back at the town house they had lounged together in bed watching half a dozen episodes of a Showtime series until falling asleep. Neither of them had brought up any conversations of significance, instead keeping it light as both tried to figure out what was wrong. But Marco knew what was wrong.

"Marco, what's wrong?" came Ophelia's voice softly from the other side of the bathroom door. Marco ran the cold water in the sink and splashed some on his face. As he patted dry with a towel Ophelia spoke. "Marco, honey, I'm okay. It was just a silly accident."

Marco shook his head. He didn't allow accidents to happen in his life. He was a professional and everything he did was with precision and purpose. He couldn't begin to fathom what was unraveling in his mind to cause the visions or hallucinations or whatever it was he was having. But the fact that they could cause Ophelia harm was of great concern to him and he had to get a grasp on it. Either that or he had to let Ophelia go.

"Marco, please--"

He opened the bathroom door to Ophelia standing there in front of him looking so small and fragile. She had turned on a nightstand lamp and it bathed half of her naked body in an orange glow. Her long, black hair was swept to one side and hanging draped over her right breast. She had her small hands folded in front of her well-groomed landing strip and her feet were crossed at the ankles. She looked adorable.

He embraced her in his arms, pulling her tightly into him. His arms wrapped around her back and his fingertips brushed the sides of her boobs. She let her body melt into his, her breasts pressed against his chest, her abdomen feeling his flaccid penis pressed between them. She wrapped her arms around his waist and felt his heart beating against her body.

"Come back to bed," Ophelia whispered. "I'll make it all better."

"I have to go," Marco said.

"What?" She tried to struggle free but Marco held her pressed tightly to him. "Go where? What's going on?"

He stroked her hair while pressing her face to his chest. "I won't be gone long," he told her. He didn't know this for sure, wasn't even certain if he'd ever see her again, but it seemed the right thing to say. He figured it wasn't a lie if he didn't really know.

"I want to come with you," she said.

"You can't."

"Marco, what did I do?" she cried and he felt her warm tears sliding down his chest. "Please, I'm sorry."

"It's not you, Ophelia, it's me."

She cried more. "Don't say that. That's what people say when they break up. Are you breaking up with me?" Her tears were like a faucet and he could feel the warm droplets on his stomach and then his penis.

"That's not it," he said. He hoped that was true. He knew he didn't want to break up with her but he needed to find out if being with her would hurt her more or less.

"Will you kiss me, please?" she asked after her held her long and hard.

"Of course."

"What kind of kiss was that?" Cassandra asked.

"Sorry, my mind was elsewhere," Marco said.

"Don't waste my time. Let's try it again, like maybe you're happy to see me even."

Cassandra pressed her body against Marco's. She was the same height as him in her flats and she was wearing a tight, black mini dress that reached to her knees but had a slit in the side all the way up to her hip. The front of the dress was cut in a V that went below her small breasts that could fit in champagne glasses. She had long legs, voluptuous hips, and a heart shaped ass to die for. Her light and dark brown streaked hair was perfectly styled in wavy curls just past her shoulders. Beneath her Prada sunglasses were hazel green eyes that had seen more than she'd ever tell.

Marco was wearing a Tom Ford suit, black, and an Italian blue silk shirt that Cassandra untucked out of his pants so she could slide her soft hands and long painted nails up the flesh of his sides and back. He smelled of cinnamon and wood, she of grapes and lust. Her tongue tasted of cherry, his a tingling raspberry from his Mentos candy he had been sucking on.

Now he sucked her tongue as his hands dug into her ass cheeks and he squeezed them like bread dough. Her pelvis grinded into his and his cock came alive like a snake from a charmer's basket. She pulled her head away but kept her body melded against his. "Now that was a kiss," Cassandra said.

She slipped one of her hands down the front of his pants and grasped his growing member. She helped it along with a few strokes. "Now that seems like you're happy to see me."

"I am," he said. "It's been a long--"

"Show me."

He scooped her in his arms and carried her to the large four-poster bed. He had a suite at the Bellagio overlooking the Vegas strip, a room that cost over five grand a night. Of course Cassandra cost twice that and was worth every penny.

Marco laid her on the bed's cream colored, velvety bedspread. He rolled her onto her stomach and undid the zipper at the back of her dress. She lifted her hips as he pulled it down and off her. She was wearing a tiny, white G-string that disappeared up the crack of her ass. He pulled them down her hips, out of her ass crack, and slid them off her legs. He could see a sliver of pink labia peeking out of her shaved pussy from behind.

Cassandra's red painted lips smiled at him as she looked over her shoulder. She began to roll over but Marco's hands grabbed her hips and rolled her back onto her stomach. "Oh," she said.

Marco's hands frantically undid his belt and pants and his rigid shaft poked out in front of him as he pushed his pants and boxers to his knees. His hands went back to Cassandra's ass cheeks and he spread them wide exposing her puckered asshole. He bent down and began to tongue her anus, slathering it with his saliva until it was dripping down her crack.

"Mmm," she moaned delightfully.

With one hand pulling her ass cheek to the side, he grabbed his cock with the other and guided it to her glistening asshole. The purple head of his prick squeezed between her cheeks and then disappeared inside her, the rim of her asshole gripping him tightly as he pushed deeper into her.

"Oh my fuck!" Cassandra cried as he filled her from behind. She breathed and relaxed through the pain that hurt so good. She was on her stomach with her head arched back and her mouth open and emitting sounds of "Oma! Oma!" as Marco's cock sunk fully into her. She felt his thighs rub against the back of her thighs and his abdomen push against her ass, rubbing and grinding as he growled in pleasure.

"Hooo," Cassandra moaned as his cock pulled back, the rim of her asshole feeling every vein and ridge of his cock as it slid out of her and then back into her.

"Oma" became "Om" as Marco began to fuck her ass, his hands on her ass cheeks spreading her open so he could watch his cock ramming in and out of her tight sphincter. He fucked her harder, faster, his pelvis slapping loudly against her ass.

"O! O! O!" she cried out as her fists tugged at the bedspread. A little tsunami rushed from her pussy up to her chest and Cassandra screamed blissfully.

"Yeah! Yeah!" Marco grunted, fucking her as hard as he could in the ass and then the head of his cock exploded like a volcano and it felt like warm lava flushing through his entire body as he gushed into Cassandra.

They were soaking in the suite's large Jacuzzi tub with a platter of chocolate covered cherries and a three thousand dollar bottle of Dom Perignon. Cassandra had her hair secured on top of her head which Marco thought made her look like a big parrot. Her neon pink nipples shimmered under the still water; she didn't like having the Jacuzzi jets on because it made her skin itch.

"How long have you been doing this?" Marco asked.

Cassandra thought a moment, a chocolate covered cherry being rolled across her lips. "I started two years before we met, so eight years."

"Do you ever think about quitting?"

"I figure I've got another five years until this body isn't such a hot commodity."

Marco shook his head. "You could go another twenty and still be fine."

She smiled coyly as she took the treat into her mouth and then ran the tip of her tongue across her lips.

Marco wasn't giving her false flattery. She wasn't quite thirty and she had the looks of a sophisticated model that would only continue to get more beautiful and refined until she was at least fifty. And she had intelligence to go with her looks that made her a rare, desired commodity among Arab sheiks and billionaires from around the world.

"What's really on your mind?" She asked Marco.

"I found the woman I'm going to marry."

Cassandra smiled and said, "Good for you." Then she frowned and added, "Does that mean I won't see you again?"

"Depends."

"On what?"

"If I marry her or not."

"Why wouldn't you?"

"I have to give up everything."

"Everything?"

"Become a completely new man."

"Do you want to?"

"I don't know if the past will let me."

Cassandra didn't know what he did other than she'd surmised long ago that it was highly illegal. That didn't bother her seeing as her own profession was outside the law. What drew the two coming back together again and again over the years was that they were both consummate professionals. They knew they were the best at what they did and they could respect that in the other.

"I've been proposed to six times," Cassandra said.

"They weren't good enough?"

"One or two of them maybe, but it means no more of this life, no more of me. And if I'm no longer me, what is the guy who marries me truly getting? I don't know what I'd become."

"Sometimes it's necessary to become an empty vessel before one can become full again," Marco said.

"But if you empty a wine vessel and fill it with water, won't you still taste a hint of the wine?"

"Unless you break the vessel and make a completely new one, no hint of the old vessel, like it never existed."

"Easier said than done." Cassandra reached for her champagne flute, one small breast rising out of the water. Marco leaned forward and kissed her pink tip.

"It's what I must do," he said as he solidified the decision in his mind. He would return and tell Dmitri he was done.

"So, I'll never see you again?"
"No."
"Well then, let's make this a night to remember."

# CHAPTER 15

"Do you remember the first night we met?" Evan asked Charlie. They were driving through the darkness in his Lexus.

"Yeah, when you perved on me."

"Did you think it would have ever come to this?"

"I've stopped long ago trying to figure out where life is going to take me," Charlie said.

"What are you talking about? You're only nineteen."

"I've been on my own since I was thirteen. You grow up quick on the streets and learn that life isn't fair."

"Yeah, but you still have control over your own life."

"Oh really? So this is something you want to do tonight?"

"Well, no. I mean it is kind of exciting."

Charlie shook her head. "It's stupid is what it is. That cop has us wrapped around his finger making us do anything he tells us. I keep trying to think about how we can get out of it but I don't see how."

"That's why you were trying to record him?"

"That was stupid of me. It just sort of came to me as we were sitting there and he was talking."

"No, it was a good idea."

"Where is this place?" They had been driving for almost thirty minutes out of Sacramento, heading mostly south. They had looked at the property online using the satellite view but it was always different actually driving to the property and experiencing hills and valleys that weren't discerned on the 2D screen. They were going past an orange grove, at least she was pretty sure they were rows of orange trees lining the country road, and the orange glow of civilization was a few miles ahead.

"GPS says seven-point-two miles," Evan said looking at his vehicle's navigation screen on the dashboard. She had gotten mad at him putting the address they were going to burglarize into a computer device that could be retrieved by the police, but Evan had pointed out it was the police that were making them hit the place. It was hard to argue that point.

"What if we killed him?" Evan said.

"Really? You're going to kill a cop?"

"Well, no, not when you put it like that."

"How else am I supposed to put it when you say what if we kill him?"

"I don't know. We could hire a hitman."

"Know a lot of hitmen, do you?"

"No. But you see them in movies all the time."

Charlie laughed. "I knew you were going to say that. You always want to pretend life is like a movie. But it's not. This is real. Everything's not over and all wrapped up in ninety minutes."

"Hitmen aren't just in the movies," Evan said defensively. "There are programs on Discovery and TruTV. Hitmen are real."

"And expensive."

"How much do you think the jewelry's worth that we've got?"

"There's maybe a pound of gold, most of it eighteen karat. Melt value is maybe ten or fifteen grand. Not enough to hire a competent cop killer I'm sure."

"So we'll get more. It's not like we don't have the skill."

"Oh yeah," Charlie scoffed. "Our last two jobs have been so successful."

"Why do you have to be so negative?" Evan asked looking at her as they stopped at a red light.

The side of Charlie's face glowed red from the light's reflection as she said, "Because I live in the real world, not some make believe movie land."

The house was a two-story cookie cutter home in an upper middle class neighborhood. Evan wasn't as concerned about the fact that it was two stories because the cop had assured them he had eyes on the home's occupants.

"How is that possible if he said he'd be watching us while in the house?" Charlie asked after Evan got off the phone with The Detective. That's all they knew him by and when they had looked up online the owner of the house that he'd caught them in it came back registered in a woman's name: Felicia Turner.

"Because he's not working alone. Remember when he threatened us. He said 'we' have every base covered and 'we' will find you. So it's not like we could go to the police because we wouldn't know who to trust."

"I don't trust any cop and wouldn't ever go to any for help," Charlie said as she got out of the SUV.

They were in the parking lot of a Whole Foods that was about half a mile from their target home. It was a little farther than they'd like but after a drive through the neighborhood they realized there was nobody parked on the streets. They walked casually through the neighborhood, both dressed in jeans and dark colored shirts and Charlie with a small backpack on.

"What have we got, a couple of Jehovah's Witnesses?"

"At this hour on a Friday? Doubtful. Where'd they come from?"

"They turned the corner at the end of the block. How much you want to bet they were in the Lexus?"

"Did you get the license?"

"I didn't write it down, but we can review the footage. Look, there they go."

"They've got balls."

"Or they've got intel that no one's home."

The two DEA agents on stakeout in a vacant house half a block away from the Casablanca home watched as the two dark clad figures went to a gate at the side of the house and disappeared into the backyard. It was day eighteen of the stakeout of the three locations they suspected Casablanca of storing either drugs or money. Twelve agents working twelve-hour shifts in pairs had accumulated quite a bit of speculative data, but nothing yet that could get them the warrants they needed to enter the buildings.

"What do you think?" Agent Ortega asked. He was a stocky Latino of about five-eight with short, dark hair and a permanent smile that made most people uncomfortable, especially when he was angry and still smiling.

Agent Ardento was nearly half a foot taller than his stakeout partner, average build, and kept his gray hair gelled back on his pointy head. Guys liked to joke that he was the original inspiration for the Coneheads. He'd been with the DEA for twenty years, twice as long as Ortega, and he still had ten to go before retirement. "I think we sit and observe, just as we've been doing."

"But if they go into the house that could give us probable cause to enter: crime in progress."

"And get us what? Some drugs or cash? Not to mention blow our cover." Ardento shook his head. "We know he's expecting his next shipment any day, our CI is certain of that."

"We know that's not coming here," Ortega said.

"Probably not, but we've got to cover all bases. We blow one stakeout and it blows them all. Call Fargot and Rentz and get them to provide pursuit surveillance. For now let's just watch and see what these clowns do."

"What are you doing?" Evan asked standing a foot behind Charlie and trying to look over her shoulder.

"What do you think I'm doing?" she whispered. "Give me some space."

"You've got plenty of space," he said as he watched her two hands working the lock picks in the keyhole. She'd been at it nearly five minutes. "Here, let me try."

"No. Just get away," she said and jabbed him with her elbow.

"Ow!" He walked away from her and began checking the windows along the back of the house.

Charlie was getting frustrated with the lock and was about to throw in the towel. At least she got Evan away from breathing down her back. Sometimes he was like an annoying puppy always following her around, asking questions, on her heels. She also caught the way he'd stare at her when he didn't think she was paying attention; it was like he was just waiting for the opportunity to begin humping her leg. At the apartment she always made sure to take a shower before him because she could imagine the perverted things he probably did in there.

Dammit, she thought as she let up tension on the torsion bar and slid the diamond tip shaped pick out of the keyhole. Every now and then she came across locks that she couldn't pick, but it was rare, especially in single-family homes. There were hundred dollar pick proof locks homeowners could buy and pay a locksmith another hundred to have them properly installed, but it was really a waste of money when most thieves didn't know how to pick locks but they did know how to break a window or use a heavy screwdriver between the door and frame.

Charlie figured she'd give the snake rake tool one more shot and if that didn't work they'd have to find another way, like actually breaking in. She applied light pressure on the torsion bar, turning it in the same direction she would if she'd had a key. While doing that with her left hand, her right hand slid the rake back and forth in the keyhole, feeling the five spring loaded pins in the lock jiggling with her motions.

Suddenly the door swung open and Charlie's heart stopped as she stood there caught red handed. She was still holding the rake in one hand but the torsion bar hung from the keyhole. Her first inclination was to run, which was her go to solution anytime things got bad and had always served her well. But then she realized it was Evan standing on the other side of the door with a big, shit-eating grin.

"You fucking jerk!" she said and punched him in the shoulder.

"Ow!" he cried as he backed up into the house.

Charlie hit him again as her heart finally started beating again, fast and heavy. "Don't ever fucking do that again."

Evan rubbed where she'd punched him. "What, get us into a house?"

"You know what I mean. We're supposed to be working together, not scaring each other to death."

"You're the one that told me to get away. I found an unlocked window above the kitchen sink."

"Good for you," she said as she grabbed her lock picking tools and put them away. She then started moving quickly through the house. "Let's just hurry so we can get out of here."

"Slow down," Fox said as he sat back in the torn and tattered green fabric motel chair. He was naked from the waist down, his pants and underwear looped around his right ankle. He held a meth pipe and lighter in his hands and proceeded to take a hit.

Nanae watched him longingly as she sat naked on her knees between his splayed legs that almost looked black they were so hairy. Her head bobbed up and down on his rigid cock, her hands making twisting motions around the base of his member. She slowed the motions of her mouth and hands.

Fox released a large cloud of gray white smoke and leaned his head back. Nanae popped the tip of his cock out of her mouth, his member and her hands slathered in her saliva. She asked Fox, "Can I--"

"As soon as you get me off," he told her. She returned to sucking him off as his phone rang. He set the glass pipe and lighter down on the nightstand and answered the phone. "Slow it down," he said.

"Huh?" said the voice on the phone.

"Not you." He shifted his hips slightly. "Yeah, that's better. Get it." He was starting to feel really good except for this annoying phone interruption.

"Get what?" Evan asked on the phone. When he didn't get a reply, he continued. "That's the problem. We're in the house, but--"

"Yeah, I know you're in the fucking house," Fox lied. He had given the two young burglars the impression that they'd be constantly watched, just as he'd told them he'd be keeping eyes on Casablanca, which was also a lie. He had seen Casablanca pick up both of his ladies in a town car and they'd gone to Club

Six and if it was like other times, the trio would likely end up at a hotel suite, sometimes with other friends, for a little fuck fest.

"Well, uh, there's a problem," Evan said. "There's a gun safe here."

"I don't want to hear about problems. I want to hear about results." Fox was getting pissed and he could feel his cock going soft. He glanced at his phone and said, "You've got three hours to figure it out. You're fucking thieves, so act like it." He disconnected the call and tossed the phone on the nightstand.

"Goddammit, this isn't working," he said as Nanae tried to suck and squeeze life back into his limp dick. She released one of her hands from his prick, licked her finger, then slid the finger between his ass cheeks and into his anus.

"What the fuck!" Fox cried as she pushed further into him. "Hey, I don't...whoa...oh, um...oh...." Her finger stimulated his prostate and he was suddenly hard in her mouth again. Damn that felt good and all he could say was, "Next time, how about a little warning first."

"Heads up, we've got something coming out," Agent Ardento said. He had a pair of binoculars as he watched the Casablanca house. The garage door had opened and a dark blue BMW X3 SUV was backing out.

"Fargo and Rentz are still ten minutes out," Agent Ortega said hanging up his phone. "I'm going to follow them," he said as he ran to the garage door in the kitchen. As he started the white Buick and hit the button for the garage door, he called Ardento on his phone. "Which way did they go?"

"They're turning left on Kingsly."

Ortega screeched out of the driveway and raced to Kingsly. He slowed down as he came around the corner and he could see the BMW's taillights a block away. "I've got 'em," he said into the phone. "Did they empty the house that fast?"

"It was nearly fifteen minutes," Ardento said. "That's actually kind of slow for professional thieves."

"How do we know they're professionals?"

"They approached the house with confidence, got past quality locks, and then just drove away casually. Very smooth and professional."

"Maybe they just wanted the Beemer," Ortega said as he followed the car to a busy business district filled with box stores, fast food restaurants and strip malls. "Wait a second. Looks like they're stopping at a Home Depot. Yep, they're going inside."

Fifteen minutes later Agents Fargot and Rentz showed up next to Ortega at the far end of the Home Depot parking lot. One was driving an older model Durango and the other a small Honda Civic. Ortega filled them in on the car and suspects and then he returned to the stakeout house down the street from Casablanca's.

Ten minutes later they watched the BMW return to the Casablanca house. "What the fuck's going on?" Ortega asked. His phone rang and he answered. "Yeah, we've got them. They just pulled back into the garage and shut the door." He listened for a moment and then said, "Okay, will do."

Ardento looked at Ortega awaiting the update. "Fargot and Rentz are stationed outside the neighborhood ready for pursuit. The thieves, or whatever they are, loaded up the BMW with a number of unknown items from Home Depot."

Two hours and twenty-seven minutes later the BMW exited the garage with two occupants. Ortega radioed Fargo and Rentz who picked up the SUV and followed it to a Whole Foods parking lot where they watched the two subjects transfer a duffel bag and a backpack to a Lexus SUV, which they then left the parking lot in, abandoning the BMW.

Fifty-one minutes later the Lexus entered the parking lot of the Regent Inn motel and parked next to a gray Charger. The male subject from the Lexus exited his vehicle and handed the duffel bag to another male subject who exited the motel room and placed the duffel bag in the trunk of the Charger.

All of this was documented with a high definition night vision camera. The DEA agents weren't sure what was going on but they hoped this might be the lucky break they'd been waiting for.

# CHAPTER 16

Fox couldn't believe their luck. He and Sasha had been at the casino barely three hours and they were up over fifteen grand. He had told her not to go to work and to dress pretty and she'd followed his directions. She was wearing a black, strapless mini dress that accentuated her every curve. She had pulled her curly straw colored hair back, leaving only one curl framing either side of her face. With her three inch black heels she was only a couple inches shorter than Fox.

He was wearing a black Hugo Boss suit he'd purchased that afternoon. It didn't look too bad on him off the rack but he was thinking he'd take it in to get tailored. With last night's six figure score from Casablanca's place he was about ready to begin living the good life - he'd earned it.

"Yeah!" Fox cried as the dice on the craps table rolled to a stop on a hard eight. Sasha squealed and hugged him tightly as the croupier pushed almost five hundred dollars in colorful chips in front of them. Fox bent over the table and scooped up the chips and handed them to Sasha who added them to their growing stack in the chip holder.

"Let's cash these in and go to the room for a little while," Fox said.

"Are we done for the night?" Sasha asked.

"No, I just need to get off my feet for a bit."

"Can we use the Jacuzzi tub?"

"We can do a lot of things."

"Not in the ass," Sasha said.

"Baby, that felt amazing," Fox told her.

"Maybe for you."

"You just need to relax a little more."

"Fox, please."

"Okay, okay, don't start whining. We're having a nice night here."

"Yes, we are," Sasha agreed as she lay on the hotel suite's king sized bed. The covers and bedspread had been pulled back and she was naked atop the white sheets that were comfortably cool after being in the tub for almost an hour. She was lying on her stomach, as Fox had told her to, and she watched him over her shoulder as he approached the bed with his boner bouncing in front of him like a camel's head.

"Come here," he said as he stood at the edge of the bed. Fox admired her sweet ass as Sasha scooted herself backwards to him. She lifted her ass up on her knees at the edge of the bed, her smooth, shaven pussy inches from his protruding member.

Fox cupped her pussy in his hand, his thumb resting on her anus. It felt like he was holding a warm, glowing ember. He gyrated his hand and thumb gently against her.

"Fox," she said and by her tone he knew immediately what her issue was.

"It's just my thumb, relax."

"I'm still sore."

"Is it in your ass? No. So stop crying."

"I'm not cry--"

"Shush!" He slipped his finger into her moist pussy and Sasha sucked in her breath. It was followed by another finger and another until all four of his fingers were in her pink, hot hole up to his thumb. He slid his hand back and forth and she rocked her hips in rhythm with his movement.

"You like that?" he asked.

"Mm-hmm."

Fox slid his fingers almost all of the way out of her pussy and then pushed his thumb against his fingertips as if his hand were a sock puppet without the sock. He pushed his whole hand into her love hole and Sasha moaned loudly. She took him all the way to the wrist and he twisted his hand inside her as if he were turning a radio knob.

"Oh Fox, that feels so good. What are you doing?"

She was warm, wet and wrapped around his wrist and he slowly jiggled his hand within her to her moaning delight. His cock was still standing at attention in front of him and the tip glistened with precum.

"Right there," Sasha said. "Ooh, yeah-yeah. Oh Fox. Oh fuck. Oh Fox." He could feel her clench around his hand and then she was quivering and shivering, her legs tensing uncontrollably.

"Oh my fuck!" Sasha gasped when Fox slipped his hand out of her. She let her legs splay out and her hips dropped to the bed.

"Don't get comfortable yet, this ride's not over," he told her. "Get up on your hands and knees. Yep. Now move forward."

Fox got on the bed on his knees behind her. Sasha's pussy was dripping with wetness as he wrapped his fist around his cock to guide it into her from behind. He sunk into her like warm butter, both of them moaning in unison as he began to fuck her doggie style. Fox reached his hands underneath her and grabbed her large, swaying breasts. The bed rocked with his thrusting and the sounds of their bodies slapping together mingled with their grunts and groans.

"Aww," Sasha said when Fox pulled his dick out of her. He pushed her over onto her back and then straddled her chest. Sasha smiled up at him, knowing what he wanted. She pushed her tits together and Fox slid his slippery cock into her cleavage. He jerked his hips back and forth as he pushed her tits together even harder around his sliding member.

"Oh yeah, baby, come on," Sasha said as she looked up at his contorted facial features with a smile. She opened her mouth and stuck out her tongue, every now and then catching the tip of his cock as it poked out the top of her cleavage. Fox's hands were atop hers on her breasts as he titty fucked her and he felt it coming as he pumped his hips and rocked his head back and forth.

He let loose with an unintelligible "Grrr!" while at the same time letting loose a load of his thick, milky white man juice. His cum shot out between her breasts onto Sasha's chin and face and she flicked her tongue and caught some of it. Another spurt hit her cheek and the side of her neck and oozed to her earlobe. His final release was milked onto her chest and between her breasts.

Fox rolled off her and onto the mattress beside her. After a few minutes of them lying there, heavy breathing returning to normal, Sasha said, smiling, "Have you been saving that stuff up?"

"Since yesterday," Fox said.

Sasha's smile disappeared. "I haven't seen you since last week."

"No shit. A guy needs to get off more than once a week."

"You better mean with your hand."

"Or what?" Fox said looking at her. She looked like a badly topped Krispy Kreme. He didn't doubt she fucked around with guys from the strip club, though if he ever caught her she'd be sorry. He'd told her as much in the past and she said she didn't do that, he was her only man. He lied and told her she was the only woman. It wasn't entirely untrue because Nanae was an informant, so fucking her was just part of work, at least in his mind.

There were a lot of things he didn't tell Sasha because his work was on a need to know basis and most everything she didn't need to know. She liked to smoke a little weed and do some shrooms now and then, but she was adamantly against all powder, pills and crystals after losing her mother and brother - everyone close to her - from those substances. Fox kept his use, and many things, from her. He figured what she didn't know wouldn't hurt her.

Sasha pushed her fingers through his hairy chest. "You don't need anyone else, it's supposed to be you and me. You know I'll do anything for you."

"I couldn't tell the last time."

"I told you it was my first time. I tried, didn't I? You were so rough."

"I'll try to be a little gentler next time," Fox told her.

She wasn't so sure she ever wanted to try anal again, but she wasn't going to mention it now. She didn't want to start a fight, and any time you told Fox he couldn't do or have something, he'd argue the point, and oftentimes go so far as to prove you wrong.

"How much longer, Fox?"

"For what?"

"You know. Us."

"No longer. It's here."

Sasha sat up.

"You look like you've been slimed," Fox laughed.

"Your fault," she said and wiped some jizz from her face. "What do you mean it's here?"

"I mean you and I are getting out of here. I don't want you working at the club anymore."

"Really?" She couldn't believe it.

"I've got to wrap up a few things and then we're gone."

"Oh Fox!" Sasha cried and leaned to hug him.

"Aah! Get back," he said as he rolled away. "I don't want that on me."

Sasha giggled and kept moving towards him. "Why not, it's yours."

Fox laughed. "Get away." He hopped off the bed and ran through the room, Sasha chasing behind him.

"I just want a hug," she giggled.

"Go wash up," he told her. "I'm going to order us room service."

"Okay. Get us a bottle of champagne to celebrate."

Fox smacked her on the ass as she went into the bathroom and then he picked up the phone and ordered room service. Sasha showered off and then began filling the Jacuzzi tub. As she sat in the filling tub she called out to him in the other room, "Are we going back downstairs?"

"Do you want to?" Fox asked as he approached the bathroom and leaned against the doorframe watching her. She was shocked at the question, not used to being asked anything by Fox, only being told how it was going to be. She was seeing a different side of him, a side she liked and hoped to see more of.

"We've been doing really good, haven't we?" Sasha said.

"Sometimes it's best to quit while we're ahead," he said, thinking more about his score at the Casablanca house than the casino. He was tired of all the bullshit and risking his life for ungrateful citizens that only complained about police brutality and angry about their speeding and parking tickets. He was ready to kick back and live the easy life, and the four hundred thousand dollar score last night would help make that a reality. He had stored it at his stash house along with the couple of hundred he already had there in cash and drugs, he and Sasha could go anywhere.

"Where are you going?" Sasha asked as Fox walked away from the bathroom door.

"Room service will be here soon," he said as he stepped into the suite's living room. He dug in his travel bag on the coffee table and pulled out a small, zippered leather pouch. Out of the pouch came his meth pipe, lighter and a little baggie of yellowish crystals. He lit up and sucked in the white-gray smoke.

A knock came at the door and Fox blew on the end of the glass pipe to try to cool it down. After a second knock, he said, "Just a minute, I'm coming."

"Room service."

"Yeah, yeah, hold your horses." Fox touched the pipe with his fingertips, it was still warm, but he stuffed it in the leather pouch and put it in his travel bag. He was still naked but figured fuck it. He'd just poke his head around the door and have the room service cart pushed into the room.

Fox pulled back the security bar and opened the door a few inches. The door was kicked hard into him. The bottom of the door tore the skin off the top of three of his toes. The heavy wood door caught him in the knee and the side of the face, knocking him backwards onto the cool marble floor. Fox spun around to go for his travel bag eight feet away that held a compact pistol. His regular service piece was in the bedroom on the nightstand and there was no way he could make it to that.

His foot slipped in his own blood on the floor and he fell to his banged knee. He scrambled up and dove for his travel bag.

"Don't do it," a familiar voice said behind him and a boot connected with his bare ass and kicked Fox off balance away from the coffee table. He hit the floor and crashed into the wall. He spun around sitting on his ass to face his attackers.

"Baby, everything okay?" Sasha called out from the bathroom. Splashing could be heard as if she were getting out of the tub.

"Go check on her," Sergeant told Hansel who immediately headed toward the bathroom, a gun in his hand. Sergeant and Cole also held guns hanging at their sides as they stood in front of Fox.

"What the fuck's going on?" Fox demanded.

"You know, that's a really good question," Sergeant said.

A scream came from the bathroom. Sergeant and Cole glanced that way while Fox glanced at his travel bag four feet away. He shifted his weight and leaned slightly that way, ready to make the leap. Cole's hand with the gun rose up and pointed at Fox. "I wish you would," Cole said coldly.

Sergeant shook his head and walked toward the bag. He pulled the handgun out and stuck it in his waistband. "Is this what its come to?" Sergeant asked. "You're going to go for a gun on your partners?"

"I wanted my underwear," Fox said.

"Uh-huh," Sergeant said and tossed a pair of grey boxer briefs at him. Cole still had his gun pointed at Fox.

"Can I get up?" Fox said while at the same time doing so. As he pulled up his underwear Hansel stepped into the room with his hand on Sasha's arm. She was holding a yellow towel tightly to her wet body and had terror in her eyes.

"Is she in on it?" Sergeant asked Fox.

Fox shook his head. "I don't know what you're talking about but she doesn't know anything."

Sergeant looked intently at Fox and then said to Hansel, "Let her get dressed and then escort her out."

"It's okay," Fox told her as her eyes pleaded to him for help across the room. "Wait for me downstairs by the blackjack tables."

"No," Sergeant said. "The detective will escort you to the taxi stand. Bryce is going to be a little indisposed the rest of the night."

"What the fuck's going on?" Fox asked as Hansel led Sasha into the bedroom.

Sergeant nodded to the couch. "Have a seat." Fox sat on the edge of a couch cushion while Sergeant sat in a nearby lounge chair, having put his gun away. Cole remained standing holding his gun down at his side. None of the men spoke as they listened to Sasha shuffling around in the bedroom. Fox was sure Hansel was getting a good show watching her get dressed.

A few minutes later she exited the bedroom in her black mini dress and high heels with a small silver purse in her hands. "Fox," she said and moved toward him. Hansel was at her side, his gun put away, and he grabbed her arm. "Hey!" she cried trying to pull away.

"Let her go!" Fox growled as he stood from the couch. Cole's body tensed and his gun raised slightly.

Sergeant gave a shake of his head and Hansel let Sasha go. She ran into Fox's arms crying. He hugged her tightly.

"Don't worry," he told her, "it's just a little misunderstanding. I'll call you in a little bit."

"Promise?" she sniffled.

"Promise."

She kissed him on the cheek and was then followed out of the hotel suite by Hansel. After the door clicked shut Fox asked, "Where's Winters?"

"He's at your apartment, just in case we missed you," Sergeant said. "We went through the place, but didn't find it there. You're not stupid enough to have it here, are you?" He gave Cole a nod of his head and Cole went into the bedroom.

"I don't know what you're looking for," Fox said.

Sergeant told him to sit down and he did. "Everybody skims a little extra," Sergeant said. "We're dirty cops, it's what we do, even from each other sometimes. I get it, we all think we're better than the others or that we risk more or do more, so it's deserved. I've taken mine too because if shit goes down, I'm in charge so I have more to lose, am I right?"

Fox didn't answer but instead looked at Cole coming out of the bedroom. He was holding Fox's cash, which he tossed on the coffee table. "That's all there is," Cole said, "maybe twenty grand."

Sergeant looked at Fox and asked, "So where is it?"

Fox shook his head, "I really don't know what you're--"

Sergeant flipped the coffee table over, Fox's money and travel bag scattering across the floor. Fox saw his leather pouch fall out of the bag and hoped his pipe didn't break inside. He really needed to get high.

"No more bullshit!" Sergeant said, standing over Fox with his fists clenched. Cole stood ten feet away with gun in hand and eyes on Fox. "The captain's breathing down my neck because he got a call from the DEA. It turns out they've been staking out all of Casablanca's properties and last night one of them gets burglarized. They follow the thieves and who do they meet up with and transfer the goods to?"

"Who?" Fox asked.

"You ain't a fucking owl," Sergeant said pointing a finger in Fox's face, "and you ain't that wise. You jeopardized everything. Go get some fucking clothes on. We're going for a ride and you're taking us to the loot."

"Sarge, I--"

"Stop talking. I can tell you're lying because your lips are moving."

Fox went into the bedroom, Cole following ten feet behind him with gun still in hand. Fox casually got dressed and then made his way over to the nightstand. His gun was missing.

"You're not looking for this, are you?" Cole asked, lifting his shirt to show Fox's gun in his waistband.

The three of them took the elevator to the casino floor, Sergeant explaining how he smoothed it over with the captain saying it was all part of a bigger operation. But what the crew had been working on was now fucked and Fox was going to give up the goods.

Fox had admitted to nothing and when the elevator doors opened there were three old ladies waiting to get on. He mule kicked Cole, aiming for the groin but Cole twisted, not caught completely off guard and took the kick in the thigh. Fox threw two of the ladies into the elevator and Sergeant was able to keep one of them from hitting the ground as he watched Fox run and disappear into the casino.

Sergeant knew there was only one way now to take care of Fox.

# CHAPTER 17

"I'll take care of that," Evan said as he lounged on the couch in his living room. He and Charlie had been watching a Japanese gangster film on his flat screen TV but then she got up and started clearing off the paper plates and pizza box on the coffee table.

"I've got it," she told him as she stuck her fingers into the tops of the four empty beer bottles and lifted them clinking off the table. Evan winced as he sat up and she said, "Just relax. Do you want me to get you another of those heating patches?"

"We used the last one," he said as she disappeared behind the couch into the kitchen. His back and shoulders had been hurting him since he'd awakened that morning on the couch. He had strained it more than he realized the night before as he and Charlie struggled to get into the safe at the house The Detective had sent them to.

After the useless call to The Detective, Evan stood in front of the five-foot tall gun safe in the corner of the bedroom. He looked at Charlie and said, "He told us to figure it out, we have three hours."

"Figure it out?" Charlie said. "I don't know how to get into a safe."

"I've got an idea how to do it."

"You've busted into a safe before?"

"Well, no, but I've--"

"Don't even say it."

"Not everything on TV is make believe," he told her. "And what other choice do we have?"

They found the keys to the BMW X3 SUV in the garage and drove to Home Depot where they picked up everything Evan thought they'd need based on the movies and true crime TV programs he'd seen. They returned to the bedroom with a grinder, electric saw, crowbars and sledgehammer.

Evan explained to Charlie that gun safes were more for keeping family members away from guns as well as being fireproof to protect important documents, not so much as impregnable containers. "Anything that can be created by man can be defeated by man," he'd said as they went to work cutting away the outer layer of steel, prying and wrenching on the metal to expose the concrete layer that was then smashed with the sledgehammer and then cutting through the inner steel shell.

It was nearly two hours of sweaty, grueling work until the innards were bared and Charlie began pulling out bundled stacks of hundreds, fifties and twenties.

"Holy shit," Evan said as he wiped his sweaty brow with his shirtsleeve. "I've never seen this much money in my life. Have you?"

"No," Charlie said, still pulling the money out of the safe. "Start putting it in the duffel bag. We've been here way too long."

"Don't you want to count it?"

"What difference does it make? We don't get to keep it."

Evan began to stuff the money in the black duffel bag they'd purchased at Home Depot. Charlie pulled the last bundle of money out of the safe and dropped it on the pile on the bedroom floor. The bedroom was a mess with the tools scattered all over the place and chunks of concrete and concrete dust caking everything.

As the duffel bag began to fill Evan looked at Charlie and said, "Do you think The Detective knows how much is in here?"

"How could he?" Charlie asked.

"That's what I was thinking."

"I was kind of thinking the same thing."

"Where's your backpack?"

Charlie got her backpack and crouched down next to the dwindling pile of bills. "Are you sure?" she asked, looking at Evan. "If he finds out, we're toast."

"He's already got us by the balls or," he looked at Charlie's crotch.

"The cunt hairs?" she finished for him. "Well that's where he's wrong because I don't have any." Evan blushed and Charlie continued, "So obviously he doesn't know everything." Charlie began stuffing bills into her backpack.

When all the money was gone from the floor Evan looked around and asked, "Should we pick up all the tools?"

Charlie shook her head. "Why? For one, we've been wearing gloves; two, we're working with the police; and three, I don't think whoever this money belongs to is in a position to call nine-one-one to report the crime."

"Good point," Evan said as he lifted the duffel bag and immediately winced and dropped it to the floor.

"Are you okay?" Charlie asked.

"I just tweaked something in my back or shoulder working on the safe."

"Want me to carry it?"

"No, I've got it." He lifted it with his other hand, and though it still hurt, it wasn't unbearable.

"That was pretty impressive," Charlie said as they got into the BMW to drive to his Lexus. Evan beamed with pride.

They had gone home and showered, separately, and then sat on the couch talking about what they were going to do and wondering if The Detective was done with them or not. They had counted the money that Charlie had stuffed in her backpack, seventy-four thousand dollars, and put it back in the backpack before Charlie went to sleep in his bedroom and Evan fell asleep on the couch watching a movie.

When he awoke a little before noon his back, neck and shoulders were killing him. He didn't have much in his bathroom for medicine, but Charlie found him some sort of sore muscle patch and ibuprofen and he'd dozed off and on as he lay on the couch watching movies.

They ordered pizza in the evening and each had a couple beers, about the only thing left in Evan's refrigerator. He'd made a crack about being arrested for contributing to the delinquency of a minor and she smacked him in the arm and then apologized profusely when he winced in pain.

After Charlie cleaned off the coffee table, she went to the bedroom and when she returned she was dressed to go out.

"Where are you going?" Evan asked, wincing as he sat up on the couch.

"I'll be back in a few minutes," she told him.

"No, you don't have to go anywhere."

"Relax, I'll be right back." Before he could protest further, Charlie slipped out the apartment door. Evan's eyes darted to the loveseat where the backpack full of money sat. It was still there. He relaxed a little, but not much. He constantly feared that Charlie might up and leave at any moment and he didn't know what he'd do.

They had discussed leaving the state for a while; give everything time to cool off. They figured that now that The Detective had gotten what he wanted he might leave them alone, or at least not pursue the matter much if they weren't around. Out of sight, out of mind was Evan's theory.

Charlie wasn't so sure, more for Evan's sake than hers. Evan still had family and a reason he'd have to return whereas Charlie would be fine if she never saw Sacramento again. She was good at running and hiding. More than once as she sat and watched him sleep she considered collecting her things and slipping out of the apartment and disappearing. But she was afraid of the situation it would leave Evan in; she at least had a little experience dealing with scumbags whereas Evan's only knowledge came from movies. And of course he had saved her life. And maybe, just a little, she kind of liked him.

Evan didn't like her leaving the way she did and he got a sinking feeling in his stomach. He got up from the couch, all of his body aching. It was as if his sore neck, back and shoulders had infected the rest of his body causing it to ache when it turned or bent. Though it was probably just because he'd been lying around and sleeping on his couch, compounding the aches from tearing open the safe.

He walked down the hallway to his bedroom. Charlie's things were scattered everywhere, her suitcase open against the wall. Evan went to his dresser and pulled the bottom drawer completely out, having to take a deep breath as pain shot through his back and shoulder.

He stuck his hand inside and lifted the flat, hidden panel he had built into the dresser's bottom. Inside was the money and jewelry that he and Charlie had accumulated from all of their previous burglaries. He was afraid maybe she had taken the stash before leaving the apartment, but now was certain she was coming back... well, pretty certain.

He put the drawer back and then looked around the room one last time. His eyes stopped on the bed where she had been sleeping the past couple of weeks and he had a brief flash of himself smelling her pillow and smelling her on the sheets. The sound of the key in the apartment door shook him out of his pervy thoughts and he rushed out into the hallway.

Charlie stepped into the apartment carrying a small CVS pharmacy bag. She looked at Evan in the hallway.

"Going to the bathroom," Evan said, his hand reaching for the bathroom doorknob.

"Need help?" she asked.

"Real funny," he said as he stepped into the bathroom thinking of when he'd helped her in there. Damn, I should have said hell yeah I need help. The thought got him a little hard and made taking a leak a challenge. With his cock in hand he considered jerking one out - it had been a few days - but he knew Charlie was out there waiting for him, or at least he imagined she was, which of course kept him semi-hard in his hand. It would probably only take him ninety seconds and surely help him relax a little more, he thought as he began to work his prick with his fingertips.

"Evan, come out here," Charlie called from the living room.

He pulled up his sweats and they bulged slightly in front of him. He tried to think of anything non-sexual as he washed his hands, but was having little luck. He grabbed a hand towel and dried his hands and then held the towel casually in front of his bulge that hadn't subsided.

"Come sit down," Charlie said. She was sitting on the couch and paying more attention to a small container in her hand than to Evan with the towel he was trying to nonchalantly hold in front of his crotch.

"What's that?" he asked as he started to sit beside her on the couch.

"No, sit here," she said. Charlie was sitting all the way back on the couch with her legs spread and was patting the cushion in front of her crotch. "And take off your shirt."

Evan turned his back towards her so she wouldn't see his chub as he pulled off his t-shirt. He sat tentatively on the edge of the cushion in front of her. "What's that, some sort of lotion?"

"It's Tiger Balm," she told him. "It's amazing for aches and pains."

Her hand touched his shoulder and he flinched. "Relax," she told him. Her hand was cool and slick with ointment and she began to slide it over his shoulder. Her other hand joined in on his other shoulder. "You're so tense and stiff," Charlie said. If you only knew, Evan thought as the towel in his lap rose higher the more she touched him.

"Scoot back a little and try to relax," she said.

Evan did so, his hips now rubbing against the insides of her thighs in her skintight yoga pants. He felt her tits brush against his back more than once as she rubbed the Tiger Balm on his shoulders and arms. Whatever medicine was in the rub was doing wonders for the muscles in his back, shoulder and arms. But one muscle of his was as tense and strained as could be.

"How's that feeling?" Charlie asked.

"Like heaven," Evan answered barely above a whisper. He wondered if there was a sedative in the Tiger balm or if it was just the soothing motions of her touch that was making him feel drowsy. He could barely keep his eyes open, even when he sucked in his breath as her hands dipped into his waistband putting ointment on his hips and lower back. The last thing he remembered were her hands on his chest.

"Wake the fuck up!"

Evan opened his eyes to see The Detective standing over him next to the couch. The TV was on behind the dirty cop, the sound on mute, no other lights on in the dark apartment. "You're doing it wrong, you fucking pansy, you're supposed to be behind her," the cop said.

It was then Evan realized Charlie was lying behind him on the couch, her body pressed against his, her arms hugging him around his bare chest. Evan sat up and realized something else: Charlie was topless except for her bra. The Detective's eyes also didn't fail to notice.

"What are you doing here?" Evan asked.

"Did you talk to the DEA?" The Detective asked.

Evan wiped sleep from one of his eyes. "What?"

"Don't fucking what me," the cop said and backhanded Evan in the side of the head. "What the fuck did you tell the feds?"

Charlie had started to get up but The Detective told her to stay where she was. He smacked Evan again. "Tell me what you told them."

"I didn't tell anybody anything," Evan said as he rubbed his head.

"We haven't seen anyone," Charlie seconded.

The Detective pointed at her and said, "If I want your opinion I'll give it to you."

"It's not opinion, its fact," she replied.

He raised his hand and stepped toward her but Evan put his body in the way. "It's true. We brought you the money and then came here. We haven't seen anyone but you."

The cop's hand lowered and he asked, "Were you watching to see if you were being followed?"

"Why would we?" Evan asked. "We assumed as much because you said we'd be being watched."

"Fucking great," The Detective mumbled as he rubbed the back of his neck. He walked to the loveseat and both Evan and Charlie tensed. The cop picked up the backpack and dropped it beside the chair as he sat down. Evan and Charlie quickly looked at each other which The Detective didn't see as he stared at the floor.

"Okay, here's what's going to happen," The Detective said. "You don't leave this apartment and don't talk to anyone. Stay off your phone and wait for my call. When I call you, be ready to go to the address I give you." He was pretty sure the other members of his crew skimmed and squirreled away money just like he did - the Sergeant had even admitted it - but he doubted they were as smart as him to have a stash house registered to someone else.

"We've already done your dirty work," Charlie said. "We're even."

The Detective jumped up. "There's no even in this game. You'll do what I say when I say."

"Typical dirty cop," Charlie mumbled.

The Detective lunged for the couch, knocking Evan to the floor and grabbing Charlie by the neck and lifting her off the couch. Her eyes bulged wide and her hands grasped the cop's hairy, muscular forearm.

"Let her go!" Evan cried as he jumped up and swung a fist at The Detective. The cop ducked and weaved and Evan's fist glanced off the bulky man's ear.

The Detective did as Evan had demanded, dropping Charlie to the floor gasping for air. He spun and punched Evan with a one-two to the body and sending Evan unconscious to the floor with an uppercut.

The cop pointed at Charlie and she cringed. "Be ready for my call," he said and left the apartment.

When Evan came to his head was on Charlie's lap on the living room floor and she was holding a towel with ice to his chin. He looked up at her in her baby blue bra and gave her a weak smile. She returned the same.

"I want to kill him," Evan mumbled through his swollen jaw.

# CHAPTER 18

"I'm done killing," Marco said. "Find someone else."

"That's not possible," Dmitri replied. "The money has already been paid. Quarter of a million."

The two men were at the New Orleans zoo standing in front of the lion exhibit. Two of the majestic beasts were lounging in the sun while three cubs romped around together near a thick tree.

Marco shook his head. "For that amount you can surely find someone else."

"For that amount you're the only one and you know it," Dmitri said. He looked around to make sure no one was in earshot. "It's a cop, it has to look natural, and it has to be done tomorrow."

Marco walked away from the lion exhibit and Dmitri followed behind him. He was tall and slender, in his late fifties and had a silver handled cane in his right hand to compensate for the permanent injury to his right leg. Marco kept his pace slow. They arrived at a large cage the size of a three-story house filled with birds and foliage.

After a family of five left beside them, Marco said, "I'm retired."

"You should have told me."

"I'm telling you now."

"You might be retiring, but I'm not. How will it make me look? I can't take the money for something like this and not produce the promised results. You know this."

Marco watched a brightly colored bird soar across the cage.

"You're really retiring?" Dmitri asked.

"I'm not retiring. I'm retired."

"After this job. It's already in your account and there's already a car being placed at the airport."

"Which airport?"

"A small landing strip southwest of Sacramento."

Marco looked at him hard. "You're picking my landing spots now?"

Dmitri put his left hand on Marco's shoulder. There weren't many men who could place a hand on him and live to tell about it. "We've been doing this a long time," Dmitri said. "I'm making it as easy as possible for you."

"If it's so easy, you do it."

Dmitri squeezed his shoulder and smiled.

"Shit," Marco said running his fingers through his hair. "I'm proposing to my girl tonight."

"Would that be the beautiful lady Maggie told me about?"

Marco nodded.

"So postpone it and ask her tomorrow night."

"I can't. I have something special planned for tonight."

Dmitri reached into his suit pocket and palmed a small flash drive which he dropped into Marco's suit pocket when no one was looking.

"I could fly out tonight," Marco said, more to himself than Dmitri. "Be there by sunrise. As long as the intel is good it could be done, but I don't like it."

"The intel's good. It's someone close to the target."

"Is that supposed to make me feel better?"

"Since when was this line of work about feeling better?"

"This is the last one," Marco said turning to Dmitri. "You won't see me again after this." He turned and walked away.

"What? You're not going to invite me to the wedding?" Dmitri called after him.

"It sounded to me like your mother wanted a big wedding," Marco said as he and Ophelia walked hand in hand along the edge of the harbor overlooking the gulf.

Ophelia smiled. "All this wedding talk for a girl who doesn't even have a ring." She was joking of course but she also felt something was up because Marco had been acting strange all afternoon. When she had tried to initiate sex at the town house Marco had promised he'd make it up to her but they had to go.

The exquisite French restaurant they had dined at was nearly empty so she didn't understand why their reservation time was so important. And then he'd whisked her outside in the dark along the ocean's edge.

"You know I told you the time had to be just right," Marco said. "It's kind of like that," he said as he pointed out into the gulf. "Like you're waiting for your ship to come in."

Ophelia looked out across the water at the few different ships and yachts in the dark water. "Kind of like how you were waiting for my ship to come in when you were in Miami?" She turned and smiled at him.

He smiled and nodded his head toward the water. She looked back out at the ships and her jaw came unhinged. The sides of three yachts were lit up in bright white lights spelling out the words: Marry Me Ophelia.

"I've waited a lifetime for this ship to come in," Marco said beside her.

"Oh Marco!" she turned to find him on one knee and holding a small jewelry box with a large diamond ring in it.

"Say you'll be mine."

"Oh yes!" she cried as she hugged him to her, pulling him tight against her belly. She looked back out over the water to read the message again through tear filled eyes. "Yes! I do!"

"No!" Dmitri cried. "I don't... you have the wrong guy."

"Wrong answer, Dmitri," the masked man said. He swung Dmitri's cane over his head and brought it down hard on Maggie's midsection. She was lying on the bedroom floor with her hands and feet bound by zip ties and wearing an elegant green dress that she had intended to wear out with her husband.

Maggie screamed in pain and if felt like the cane had ruptured something inside her as she curled up in the fetal position, coughing and crying.

"Please, stop!" Dmitri begged. He was on the floor five feet away from his wife, his hands and feet also bound with zip ties.

He also had a nasty bump on the back of his head from when he'd been knocked unconscious before being zip tied. He had returned home from his meeting with Marco and when he'd walked into the bedroom he froze in shock seeing Maggie on the floor and then he was hit from behind and it was lights out.

Dmitri didn't know how long he'd been out before the masked man had slapped him awake and asked him about Marco. Except the masked man didn't mention the assassin by name, only as "the man you hired." Dmitri needed to find out how much this intruder knew and what it was the guy wanted to know before he'd be able to figure a way out of this predicament. The fact that the intruder was wearing a mask was a good sign that Dmitri and his wife could get out of this alive.

The masked man dressed all in black poked Dmitri with his own cane and asked, "Where can I find the man you hired?"

Dmitri shook his head. "You can't find him. It's impossible. I can't find him. All contact is established online through anonymous servers."

Maggie was looking at her husband with tears and pain and fear in her eyes. She had no idea what her husband was mixed up in and she was sure the home invader had to have the wrong house.

"Nothing is impossible," the masked man said. "I found you, didn't I?"

Dmitri shook his head again. "I don't know you. I don't think you--"

The masked man spun around and swung the cane as if it were a nine iron and he was hitting a golf ball a couple hundred yards. Instead he hit Maggie in the forehead and there was an audible crack as her head snapped back, her eyes rolled back in her head and bright red blood streamed from her head onto the tan carpet.

Dmitri screamed hysterically. "Maggie! No! Maggie! Maggie!" He tried to squirm his body across the floor closer to her but the masked man pushed his foot against Dmitri's chest. "She has nothing to do with this!" Dmitri screamed at the invader. He kept looking at his wife trying to determine if she was still alive or not. "Who are you?"

"I'm the cop who hired you to kill the other cop."

"I don't understand."

"It's complicated. And it's going to get even more complicated. That's why I need a leash on your hitman."

"I have nothing I can tell you," Dmitri said. "I am just a middleman."

The masked man bent down and laid the cane upon Dmitri's neck and slowly added pressure as he spoke. "Let me tell you something, Dmitri. I used to do a little black bag work in the military and I've kept a couple contacts in the alphabet agencies. That's how I was able to get a jet to fly here and have this meeting with you and how I also know you made two calls to Sacramento after accepting payment for the assassination. What arrangements did you make?"

Dmitri struggled to breathe as the cane crushed against his trachea. "It... was... unrelated," he gasped.

The masked man pulled the cane away as he stood. "I don't believe you," he said simply. "I'll give you a minute to rethink your answer." He walked out of the room, leaving Dmitri wheezing for air.

"Maggie," Dmitri croaked. "Maggie, are you okay?" She didn't respond as she lay in the blood pooled around her head and breasts. Dmitri wiggled his body towards her, getting within a foot before the masked man returned to the bedroom.

"Tell me what arrangements you made in Sacramento," the masked man said. He was holding the cane by the bottom, as he had when he swung it at Maggie's head. The silver tipped handle was glowing an angry orange from being held over the open flame of their gas stove.

"No!" Dmitri screamed, not in answer to the question but rather to the pain of the heated cane handle being pressed against the side of his cheek and into his left eye socket. His skin seared and bubbled and his eyeball boiled and burst.

The masked man only had to heat the cane twice more before learning about the waiting car for the hitman at a small unmanned airstrip outside of Sacramento. Before leaving the Louisiana country estate the masked man set fire to the house.

"You are so hot," Marco said and then kissed Ophelia deeply, his hands sliding up her back and over her ass. They were standing next to the king sized bed in his town home. Their tongues touched and tangled tenderly and Ophelia's arms hugged her fiancé tightly to her.

"Oh Marco," she sighed as he pulled away. They stared into each other's eyes and then Marco began to slide his hands down her sides while still keeping eye contact. Ophelia was wearing an elegant white dress that reached almost to her knees. Marco's warm hands moved from the fabric of her dress to her smooth calves and to the straps of her silver Prada heels. Still looking up at his wife-to-be, Marco undid one shoe and slid it from her foot and then the other.

He stayed crouched in front of Ophelia, their eyes never losing contact, and he slowly slid his hands up the sides of her legs. His hands went under her dress, the hem rising with his wrists and then his fingers were curling around the straps of her G-string on her hips. He pulled the tiny red garment slowly down her legs and she stepped out of it.

Marco stretched his arms up, lifting the hem of her dress as he did so, until he exposed her delicate pussy with its perfectly groomed airstrip. He savored her pussy with his eyes and then looked up to see her smiling down at him. He brought his mouth between her legs and Ophelia cooed as she brought her hands to his head.

Ophelia spread her legs a little wider as Marco's tongue wiggled up and down the crack of her pussy. She moaned as he gently shook his head side to side, his tongue brushing across her clit and then his whole mouth was upon her and grinding into her. He felt so good and Ophelia began to pulsate her pelvis against his face as he pleasured her pussy.

"Oh, Marco," she gasped as his tongue twisted and twirled in between her pink pussy lips. Her breaths were short and fast as she neared the edge of ecstasy, ready to fall into the abyss of orgasmic bliss. "Don't stop!" she panted.

Marco's hands grasped her bare ass, squeezing and spreading her ass cheeks as his tongue spread her pussy lips. Her dress had fallen over his head and shoulders but she was no longer looking at him anyway as her head jerked back and forth. He clung to her ass, holding her to his face as her pelvis began to shake and quiver.

Ophelia cried out as if she were falling as orgasms poured down her body like a heavy summer rain. Her knees went weak and she clung to Marco's head for support, her pussy pressed against his face for balance. She screeched when his tongue brushed her sensitive clit and she dug her fingers into his hair and pushed his head away.

Marco rose up from underneath her dress, his hands still holding onto her wobbly body. He undid the zipper at the back of her dress and she put her hands to her sides to let the garment fall to the floor. His fingers deftly undid the strapless red bra that matched her panties and it was dropped onto the heap on the floor.

He cupped both of her breasts in his hands and sucked on one pebble hard nipple and then the other. Ophelia was undoing the buttons of his emerald silk shirt but was slow going as she found herself lost in the sensations of his mouth. She got his shirt unbuttoned and then reached for his black slacks but couldn't quite reach them.

"Come here!" she growled as she dropped to her knees in front of him. She could see his hardness straining the fabric of his pants and she began to tug at his belt. Marco bent down and grabbed her face in his hands and he kissed her deeply, longingly; she felt like she could melt into a big puddle at his feet.

Marco put his hands on his belt but Ophelia pushed them away. She got his belt undone and then his slacks were unclasped and unzipped and falling to his ankles. His blue silk boxers were pulled down right behind them and Marco's rock hard cock was poking out in front of him and caressing Ophelia's cheek. She grasped his veiny member in two hands as she opened her mouth wide and slid him into her.

"Oh, baby," Marco moaned as Ophelia slathered his cock with her wet, warm mouth. She slid the length of him into her until he almost touched the back of her throat. One of her hands stroked his cock while the other cupped and squeezed his balls. Her rhythm was slow and deliberate and he pushed his fingers through her hair as he watched her giving him head. She looked up at him and smiled with her eyes.

After five minutes of sucking, Ophelia's lips were swollen and numb but she didn't stop until Marco said, "Come up here," and pulled her up to him. He helped her onto the bed as he slipped his shirt from his shoulders. She lay on her back, propped up on her elbows, watching him with her legs spread in welcome. Marco stepped out of his shoes, pants and boxers, the entire time his eyes bouncing from Ophelia's eyes to her pussy and back. She was licking her lips as her man got on the bed and climbed atop her.

"Yes, Marco," she breathed into his ear as his thick cock pushed in between her raised legs. Her pussy was tight, wet and warm as it engulfed him. "Oh yes," she sighed as his hips began thrusting back and forth and they gazed into each other's eyes. Marco's arms were out in front of him on either side of her, propping him above her as their hips slapped together. Ophelia put her hands upon his chest, his face, his shoulders. Her hips thrust to meet his own and then their movements became frenzied.

"Marco!" she cried and clung to him as orgasms moved through her like earthquakes. Marco grunted and gasped loudly as he exploded like a geyser inside her, filling her with his hot fluid. Their bodies continued to buck and rock together until Marco collapsed atop his fiancée, their sweat covered bodies melding together.

After an undetermined amount of time Marco went to roll off of her but Ophelia hugged him tight to her and squeezed her pussy muscles to keep his penis from escaping. "Don't go yet," she said. He relaxed and lay atop her feeling her breasts squished beneath his chest, her silky smooth legs rubbing against his.

"I have to fly out tonight," Marco said.

"Take me with you," Ophelia told him.

# CHAPTER 19

"You can't come with me," Charlie told Evan. "You've got family and ties here."

"It's my life," Evan said, "I can do what I want."

"But what if The Detective goes after your parents or something?"

"I'm not going to live my life being scared of him."

"Um, that's kind of why we'd be running."

"You know what I mean."

"I think you're maybe still a little dazed," Charlie said. They were both lying in his bed and she rolled off to the side and stood up and stretched. Daylight came through the bedroom window and highlighted her figure. She was in a pair of red shorts and a white t-shirt and as she stretched Evan could tell she wasn't wearing a bra. He wondered where the baby blue bra was that he last saw her in. Thinking of her taking off her bra and seeing the indent of a nipple in her t-shirt caused a stirring down below and Evan rolled onto his side so as not to poke the blankets up.

"Did you sleep with me last night?" Evan asked.

"We didn't sleep together."

"No, I mean--"

"I stayed in bed with you to make sure you didn't have a concussion," Charlie said as she went to her suitcase.

"I'm okay," Evan said. He touched his jaw and winced and there was a dull ache in his head. "People get punched all the time."

Charlie was pulling things out of her suitcase and Evan's cock got harder as he watched the fabric of her clothing strain against her skin. "Do you?" she asked.

"Huh?"

"Get punched all the time?"

"Well, no. The last time I got punched was in college for talking to some drunk's girl. He said I touched her boob."

"Did you?"

"Not on purpose."

"You're such a pervert," Charlie said as she held some jeans, a shirt, bra and panties in her arms. "I'm going to take a shower."

Evan had full morning wood going on, especially thinking of Charlie getting in the shower. It was then that it struck him that he was only wearing his boxers beneath the covers. "Hey," he said as Charlie reached the door, "did you undress me?"

"I just removed your pants," she said as she exited the bedroom.

"That's undressing. Who's the pervert now?"

"Shut up," Charlie said from the hallway before shutting the bathroom door.

Evan rolled over in the bed and buried his head in her pillow. She smelled so good, like pink flowers and bubblegum. He grinded his hips into the mattress as he heard the shower going and imagined Charlie naked and the water running down her body. He pictured her shaved pussy as he moved his hips back and forth atop the mattress while squeezing her pillow to his face.

He was pulled out of his masturbating fantasy by the sound of his phone ringing in the living room. "Shit," he mumbled as he got out of bed. His boxers bobbed with his hardness as he walked down the hall and he was glad Charlie was in the shower. Of course then he fantasized about her seeing his protruding boxers and inviting him into the bathroom with her and her helping to pull the boxers off of him.

His phone continued ringing as it sat on a small table near the front door. Charlie must have plugged it in last night for him. The phone showed: Unknown Caller.

"Hello?" Evan said.

"About fucking time," the angry voice on the other end said. "I told you to stay by the goddamn phone."

It took Evan a moment to realize who it was.

"Do you have a pen and paper?" The Detective asked.

Evan looked around. "Um, yeah, just a sec."

Before Evan found the necessary implements the cop was giving him an address. Luckily Evan had a better than average memory but he still looked for something to write it on. "It has to be today," The Detective said, "and there's a chance there will be somebody home."

"Whoa, hold on. We don't do that."

"You said you didn't know how to do safes either. Figure it out!"

Fox thought he had it all figured out. He had put a GPS tracking unit on the white Toyota Avalon that had been parked at the airstrip. He had followed it in real time on his computer and mapped it to a nice suburban home north of downtown later in the day. He'd received a text alert notifying him that the vehicle was moving and he monitored it on his computer, pretty certain the hitman was on his way to do what he had been paid to do.

Twenty-five minutes later Fox pulled into the driveway of the two story suburban home. It was on a quiet street that had homes lining one side of it and the other side of the street was lined with trees and shrubbery and a chain link fence that encircled a water management reservoir. Two houses down a gray haired lady in a large straw hat and gardening gloves paid him no mind as she plucked weeds from a flower bed alongside her driveway.

Fox stepped out of his gray Charger wearing jeans, a white dress shirt and a blue blazer a couple shades darker than his jeans. He walked toward the front door carrying the silver headed cane at his left side like it was a baton. Before reaching the front door he saw movement inside the house and it gave him pause. Was the hitman still inside and someone else driving the car with the tracker? Or had the hitman merely stopped at this house for an errand or such and it wasn't where he was staying? It was certainly possible the hitman was planning on doing the hit and leaving the same day and not staying at any location. If that were the case Fox would have to revamp his entire plan.

Fox continued his trek to the front door - as they'd say on the poker table, he was already pot committed so he had to at least play out this hand. He rang the doorbell with his left hand while slipping his right hand inside his jacket. He heard the bare feet on a hardwood floor and then the door was opened by a beautiful Middle Eastern woman a couple inches shorter than Fox. She was wearing a flimsy orange dress that didn't quite reach to her knees. It had spaghetti straps holding the thin fabric over her braless breasts that were barely half covered.

"Yes?' she asked unassumingly, a slight smile on her lips.

Fox pulled out his wallet and flashed his gold detective badge. "I'm Detective Fox with the Sacramento Sheriff's Department. Can I ask who you are please?"

"What is this about?" she asked, her smile gone.

"There has been a situation. Can you tell me, are you the owner of this house?"

"What situation?" She had a worried look on her face.

"Ma'am, can you please answer the question."

"This is just a vacation rental. Oh no, has something happened to Marco?"

"Who is Marco to you?"

"He's my fiancée."

"Can you describe him to me."

The beautiful lady gave Fox a description that matched the description Dmitri had given him. "What happened, is he all right?" the woman asked.

"Was Marco driving a white Toyota Avalon?"

"Um, it was a white car, I think. I didn't really pay attention. It was waiting for us at the airport."

Inwardly Fox smiled but he kept his face stern and serious. "Ma'am, I'm going to need you to come with me."

"Oh god, what is it? What happened to Marco?"

"I'll explain when we get downtown, but we need to go now."

"I have to get my purse. And my shoes," she said and quickly departed the foyer. Fox stepped inside and leaned the cane against the wall. When the woman returned she was wearing white flats and carrying a small silver purse. "Please tell me he's okay," she said as they exited the house. She didn't see the cane leaning in the corner nor the note attached to it that had a phone number and message that read: Call before making your next move.

Marco's next move was critical as he watched Sergeant Jake Mellanski walking across the busy street after leaving the chain coffee store. He would like to have been able to run him down in the street, make it look like an accidental hit and run, but because Dmitri had arranged for the Toyota Avalon he was driving, he had reservations not knowing how it might be linked to his handler.

Marco watched the sergeant get into his white Ford Explorer and he followed a few car lengths behind. If the intel he had studied was correct, he knew where the cop would be going to next, and it seemed they were heading in the right direction according to the Garmin GPS unit that was suctioned to the windshield with its wire dangling to the lighter socket that nobody ever used for lighters anymore.

The Explorer drove for about five miles before turning into the parking lot of U.S.A. Fitness. Marco drove past the large building with less than a quarter of the parking lot in use. He took the first right and quickly went around the block, pulling into the gym's parking lot in time to see the sergeant go through the front door.

Marco parked at the edge of the lot farthest from the building to avoid his vehicle showing up on any security cameras. He reached into the backseat for the white ball cap and the small gym bag he'd purchased before beginning his surveillance operation. He got out of the car and walked toward the fitness center.

He knew it wouldn't be easy, but if he missed his chance here it would get really tricky because the sergeant would be starting his shift and he'd be in the constant vicinity of law enforcement officials. So he had to make this work because there might not be another open window of opportunity. But first he'd have to get past the front desk workers utilizing a ploy.

    The ploy Evan and Charlie had come up with involved them wearing identical button up white shirts and red ball caps. Evan was carrying a cheap sprayer and Charlie a clipboard as they walked up the steps of the single story home. If anyone answered the door they would play it off that they were from an exterminating company and Charlie would attempt to distract the occupant while Evan attempted to look around. It was a piss poor plan but all they could come up with on short notice.

    Charlie rang the doorbell at the front door of the large home while Evan glanced nonchalantly around. It was a good sized home with a decent sized front yard that sloped slightly to a sidewalk and then a busy street. There were similar single story homes on either side and across the street and what people were out or moving around were paying them no mind. Charlie knocked on the door and then said, "Let's go around back."

    "Looks like we lucked out," Evan said as they opened a wooden gate at the side of the house and went into the backyard.

    "We're not inside yet," Charlie replied.

    They stepped onto a back patio and Charlie handed Evan her clipboard and removed her lock picks from her pocket. He reached past her and tried the doorknob and it opened. He smiled at Charlie.

    She put her picks away and said, "I don't like it when doors aren't locked. It gives me a bad feeling."

    "Lots of people forget to lock up or think someone else locked the door. Come on," Evan said as he stepped into the house.

    They were in a large kitchen with new stainless steel appliances and granite countertops. The kitchen opened to a large dining room that they moved through without interest and came to a living room with a large orange sectional couch taking up almost half of the space. On the other side of the living room were the front door and a hallway and someone walking down the hallway.

Charlie dropped behind the back of the couch and pulled Evan down behind her. They peeked over the top of the couch to see a wet woman with a pink towel wrapped around her midsection and leaving a trail of water droplets behind her. She was maybe an inch or two taller than five feet and her shoulder length blonde hair was dripping down her back.

The woman of the house reached for the front door and her towel fell to the floor. "Dammit," she said as she bent over baring her slightly larger than average ass to Charlie and Evan. Charlie felt Evan shifting behind her and then felt something poking her in the back. Across the living room the woman held the towel in front of her as she opened the door an inch and peered outside. "What the...?" she said grumbling as she closed the door and turned back down the hallway from where she came.

When the woman had gone Charlie pushed Evan away and whispered, "You are such a pervert!"

"What? It wasn't me, it was the sprayer," he whispered back and holding up the sprayer to show her.

She glanced at his crotch and could see he was hard. Evan blushed and said, "What do you expect, she was completely naked. Let's get out of here."

"No, we're already here. Come on."

They tiptoed down the hallway following the trickle of water that disappeared behind a closed bathroom door. There was splashing and talking and the faint sound of music coming from the other side.

"She's in there with someone," Evan whispered.

Charlie shook her head. "She's on the phone. I'll check the house and you stay here and listen to make sure she stays in the tub."

"Why am I the one staying here?"

"Because you're the pervert."

The first thing Sergeant thought was the guy must be a pervert. Not that he had a problem with homos, there were a few that were on the Sacramento Sheriff's Department roster, but that didn't necessarily mean he liked sitting naked alone in a room with one.

Sergeant was sitting on a wooden bench in the sauna room wearing nothing but a small white towel around his waist. He liked hitting the gym during the middle of the weekday when most people were still at work and the gym was usually pretty empty. The detective was leaning with his head back against the wall when the dark haired, tan skinned man walked in also wearing only a white towel. Sergeant popped open one eye and then shut it again as the newcomer added more water to the hot rocks which in turn filled the room with even more thick steam.

Three walls of the benches lined the room making a square U around the heated rocks and the wooden entrance door. Sergeant heard the man sit down and felt the bench he was sitting on move with the new weight. Through the thick steam he saw the man sitting within arm's reach of him. Having worked in law enforcement for over sixteen years, he knew the world was filled with every sort of freak and they'd even busted a gay bathhouse once in a joint operation with the city police.

Feeling a little uncomfortable but also having sat in the steam long enough, Sergeant stood up and stepped away from the bench. The room was still thick with steam and he heard the man before he saw him. When he did see him, he thought the man was reaching for his towel and Sergeant instinctively clasped his hands to the towel around his waist.

The man was quicker than Sergeant imagined and before the full threat reached the fight or flight portion of his brain it was too late. The man kicked one of the detective's legs out from underneath him while at the same time the full force of the man's momentum was driving the cop's head into the steel corner of the container holding the hot rocks.

Sergeant's blood sizzled on the rocks as his body lay motionless on the sauna floor, his blood escaping his gaping head wound and seeping into the moist wood slatted floor.

Marco checked for a pulse that merely fluttered briefly and then was gone. He quickly dressed and disappeared before anybody else came.

# CHAPTER 20

Nanae wished he'd come already. Fox had been fucking her hard for nearly thirty minutes and her pussy was hurting like a sonofabitch. She had tried to tell him that she was still having problems down there, but once the detective was all cracked out there was no reasoning with him.

She liked him better when he was on meth. Well, like was a strong word - maybe tolerated was a better one. But he did kind of look out for her and he was always getting her high and he'd made sure she hadn't been busted in months, so it all seemed a fair trade off. But when Fox was on crack there was no talking sense to him and any little thing could send him flying off the handle.

So Nanae remained on her back with her legs spread as Fox pounded atop her, his cock ramming in and out of her sore pussy. Her little cupcake titties wiggled back and forth with the shaking of the king sized bed. More than once she faked an orgasm but it didn't seem to be making him come any faster.

Nanae squeezed Fox's butt cheeks that were flexing and contracting as his hips bounced atop her. She slid a finger down his sweaty ass crack and then slipped said finger into his tight asshole.

"Hey!" Fox said, opening his eyes and looking at her for the first time in twenty minutes. He didn't stop fucking her, his ass cheeks squeezing against her partially inserted finger. "What did I tell you about that surprise buttsex shit."

"You like it, don't you?" she said as she pushed her finger further into his hot asshole.

"That's... not...." His hips quivered and spasmed against her as she fingered his hole and he exploded inside her. "The point," he finished saying. His cock jerked and shot more of his load into her as he collapsed his hairy, sweaty body atop hers. "I don't like surprises."

The bedroom door swung open and Sasha stood there in a red and gold mini skirt and black V-neck top accentuating her cleavage. "You fucking bastard!" she screamed. "I've been worried sick about you and this is what I get?" She spun around on her four-inch heels and stormed off down the hallway.

"Sasha, wait!" Fox said as he got off the bed, Nanae's finger still in his ass. He brushed her hand away and rushed after the stripper. "Sasha!"

"Just leave me alone," Sasha yelled as she threw open the front door and barged outside. She bumped into a pretty teenage girl with large, perky breasts and her dark hair in a ponytail. "Who are you, another one of his whores?" Sasha snarled.

Fox leaped out of the house and grabbed Sasha by her yellow corkscrew hair. He yanked her backwards toward the house and she pinwheeled her arms to keep from falling. "Let me go, you bastard!" she screamed.

Evan was standing in the yard behind Charlie and he instinctively put an arm around her waist and pulled her back. They were both slack jawed at the sight of the naked cop wrestling the woman back into the house. And try as they might, neither of them could help but look at the four-inch stream of semen swinging from the tip of The Detective's semi-hard cock.

"Get the fuck in here!" the naked cop yelled and it took a moment for Evan and Charlie to realize he was talking to them and not the woman who was now on her ass inside the house. Charlie looked around the neighborhood a little more than surprised that someone else hadn't heard or seen the commotion. Evan, on the other hand, was looking at the lady's see through sheer, black panties, exposed from her skirt riding up and her legs splayed on the floor. He also noticed one of her nipples was sticking out of the black V-neck as her shirt had become twisted and askew.

The Detective yelled at them again and both Evan and Charlie stepped into the house. "Have a seat on the fucking couch," he told them over the yelling and crying and squirming of the woman whose hair he still had in his grasp. He then dragged her backwards to the bedroom at the end of the hall and slammed the door shut.

"What the fuck," Charlie whispered as they both sat on the couch. "That guy's fucking lost it."

Evan was carrying a small green carry on suitcase in his left hand that he set on the floor. "Who do you think she is?"

"Who cares. We need to get out of here."

"I don't care who she is," Sasha growled. "I want the fuck out of here."

Fox had lifted Sasha off the floor, mostly by her hair, and was now holding her from behind in a bear hug. One of her breasts was fully exposed from her struggling and her skirt had ridden up to her hips. "How did you even find this place?" he asked her.

"You gave me the address weeks ago, you fucking high mind," Sasha said, struggling in his grasp.

Nanae was sitting up in the bed, her back against the wall, the crack pipe in one hand and the lighter in the other. As soon as Fox rushed out of the room she had scrambled to get another hit. The ache in her pussy was forgotten as the smoky, smooth sensation swished through her naked body.

"Listen to me, Sasha," Fox said, his mouth next to her ear and hot on her skin. "This bitch is nothing to me." He raised his voice to Nanae, "Tell her you're nothing to me."

"I ain't nothin' to him," Nanae said.

"I don't care," Sasha cried, tears streaming down her face. "I just want to go." She sobbed and went limp in Fox's arms.

"No," he told her, "you're staying with me. Forever from now on." He held her tight against his body and moved her toward the bed. "Come on, you just need to relax."

Sasha's heels scraped against the floor trying to push herself away from the bed. "No, I'm not getting into bed with her. No! I don't want her here."

"Get your shit and get out," Fox told Nanae. Sasha cried and kept her eyes closed and Fox continued holding her from behind as Nanae got off the bed. Nanae picked up her bra from the floor and began to slide it on. "Get the fuck out right now!" Fox growled. Nanae scooped up all of her clothes and shoes and ran out of the bedroom.

"Um, hi," Evan said as the tall, thin black woman walked into the living room buck naked.

"Hey," she said as she dropped her pile of clothes on the loveseat across from the couch. "Can you hold this?" she asked Charlie, holding out the crack pipe and lighter.

"No," Charlie said, not looking at the lady and then hitting Evan's arm when she saw his eyes glued to the lady's nakedness. "Stop being a perv," she hissed at him.

The naked woman set the pipe and lighter on the coffee table and began to get dressed, unabashedly bending over more than once just feet away. Evan didn't stare but he still caught glimpses of pink and some dark nipple, enough to make him have to shift in his seat. Charlie merely shook her head at him.

"Can one of y'all bring me home?" the woman asked after slipping on some copper colored Capri pants and an orange tank top over her black push up bra.

"No, they can't," Fox said as he walked down the hallway toward them wearing a pair of blue boxers. He saw the crack pipe and lighter on the coffee table and snatched them up. Nanae gave him a sad, puppy dog look. He gave her twenty dollars and told her to call a taxi.

"Twenty dollars ain't enough for me to get home," Nanae said.

"Then you'll have to barter with the driver," Fox told her and then turned his attention to Evan and Charlie. "What did you get?"

"There was nothing much," Evan said. "Just a little jewelry and--"

"No safe? No big cash or drugs? You didn't look hard enough."

"We know what we're doing," Charlie replied.

"Fuck. He must have a storage unit or something," Fox said, more to himself. Sergeant had practically admitted to him that he skimmed just like everyone else did. It didn't matter now and he could always maybe look for it later. He saw Evan lift up a small suitcase to hand to him and Fox waved it away. "You can keep that petty shit for your time."

"The taxi gonna be twenty minutes," Nanae told Fox eyeing the pipe in his hand.

The bedroom door opened and Sasha stormed out. She was barefoot and her shirt was untucked. "What the fuck is she still doing here?" she snarled looking at Nanae.

"She's waiting for a taxi," Fox said.

"She can do it outside."

"You heard her," Fox said to Nanae.

"We can take her home," Charlie said.

"Who the fuck are they?" Sasha asked crossing her arms and tapping her foot.

"I already told you," Fox said, "that's my niece and nephew. And they're not going anywhere. Go back to the room."

The front door opened and closed and Nanae disappeared outside. Sasha turned around and walked back to the bedroom, swaying her hips side to side. Fox turned to Evan and Charlie. "If you leave this house before I say, you know the kind of shitstorm I can rain down on you." He walked off down the hallway and disappeared behind the bedroom door.

Evan unzipped the small suitcase and pulled out a .44 Bulldog revolver taken from the burglary. "Tell me again why we can't just shoot him."

Charlie pushed his hand and gun back toward the suitcase. "We're not killers. And he's a cop. And killing a cop is all bad."

Killing the cop couldn't have gone any better Marco thought as he pulled the Toyota into the driveway of the two-story vacation rental. He didn't like that this house didn't have a functional garage - it was filled with a half built dune buggy and boxes and totes of the homeowner's junk - but it was all he could arrange on such short notice. It still beat being in a hotel and it didn't really matter because he and Ophelia wouldn't even be staying for the night.

The house was unusually quiet when he stepped in through the front door and at first he figured his fiancé must have decided to take a nap. When he didn't find her upstairs in bed or lying on the couch he assumed she must have Ubered to a local mall.

Marco got his phone from the Faraday bag that was in his suitcase. He inserted the battery, replaced the back and powered the device on. There were no messages from Ophelia, but then he wasn't expecting any. He sat down on the living room couch and sent her a text message telling her that he'd come pick her up wherever she was.

He set his phone on the coffee table and picked up the television remote. He flashed through the channels, skipping anything news related, and settled on The Carbonaro Effect.

Like magic, when Fox turned on the television, the evening news was on. Evan and Charlie were still on the couch, not having moved as they listened to the cop and the stripper in the back bedroom first fighting and then fucking. Now the cop was sitting in his boxers on the loveseat as it slowly grew darker outside and the glow of the TV seemed to get brighter inside.

Evan looked at Charlie and she shrugged her shoulders. He cleared his throat and said, "Why are we--"

"Sh-sh!" The Detective said as he waved a hand at him while turning up the volume with the remote in his other hand.

On the television screen an anchorwoman was saying something about a terrible accident at a nationwide gym franchise and giving the name of a local deputy sheriff. The cop was standing and obviously excited about what he was hearing which was evident by the smile on his face and the bulge in his boxers. He caught Charlie looking at his crotch out of the corner of his eye. He pushed his hips towards her and she cringed against the couch.

The cop chuckled. "Maybe you two would like to join us in the bedroom, have us a little foursome."

Evan had missed what just happened, watching a funny car insurance commercial, and he looked from Charlie to the cop. All that had registered in his brain was that there might be an offer of sex on the table.

"I thought you told her we're your family," Charlie said.

The Detective smiled. "So I'll tell her you're from Kentucky."

"No thanks," Charlie replied and leaned as far away as she could.

The stripper called to him from the bedroom. The cop nodded at Charlie. "You know, it might help loosen you up."

Marco was tense and his intuition was telling him something was wrong. He wasn't sure what but he knew enough to trust that little voice. He gathered up his and Ophelia's bags and brought them to the front door to load in the car. He wanted to be ready when Ophelia returned so they could go straight to the airstrip.

Marco saw the cane propped up in the corner of the foyer by the front door. He dropped both pieces of luggage and quickly drew his gun from his waistband. How long had the cane been there and why didn't he see it earlier? He was pissed at himself for slipping and not being on top of his game.

He approached the cane as if it were a live snake that might strike at any second. His breathing stopped and he was pretty sure his heart stopped beating for a few seconds when he realized who the cane belonged to and what it now meant. He pulled the note from the cane and called the number knowing that everything was bad in his world. He didn't even give a single fuck that he was calling the number from his phone rather than a burner. Right now everything in his life was a burner, to be tossed away after its one and final use. If he lost Ophelia, his only fear, then the whole world could just burn away.

A man answered and spoke on the other end of the line. Marco embedded the man's every word and voice inflection to memory because he was certain that someday, somehow, he would find this man and kill him, or worse. The man sent him a file with the names and addresses of three more cops to kill.

Marco didn't try to negotiate or bargain, he'd do whatever was necessary to have his woman back.

"Let me talk to Ophelia," Marco said.

"The only way to see or talk to her is to do what you're told."

# CHAPTER 21

"No, I told you," Detective Clive Winters told her, "extra onions and light on the peppers." He was standing at the counter of Hoagies, Heroes and Subs, a sandwich shop a couple blocks from his apartment. He'd been coming into the place almost daily since it opened almost three years ago. Yet it seemed like every time he had to explain and re-explain his order. Of course it didn't help that their turnover rate for employees matched that of the first year of Trump's White House.

Two Latino kids were working behind the counter, a boy of about eighteen at the cash register and the girl in front of him who looked barely fifteen. Her long, dark hair was tied in a ponytail and she wore a brown visor and a matching brown apron that made her figure look like a cardboard cutout. Her green nametag with gold lettering said her name was Audrey. She was intently making the sandwich, her plastic gloved hands dipping into the different containers in front of her and dropping items onto the split length of bread on the counter at her midsection.

Winters was watching her but his mind was a million miles away. He was technically on the clock but after hearing of Sergeant's freak gym accident a couple hours earlier, he made a bee line home to make sure all of his affairs were in order and that there was nothing evidently incriminating laying out in his place. He had no idea what this would mean to the crew now that Sergeant was gone. And then there was still the matter of Fox to deal with whom they were pretty certain had undercut them all by having one of Casablanca's houses hit.

None of the crew had seen or heard from him since the fiasco at the casino.

"Anything else, sir?" the girl asked as she looked up at him over the Plexiglas window that rose chin high between her and the customer. The portly man with the short black and grey hair opened his mouth and then red and gray matter was spewing out from his face covering her and the Plexiglas as well as splattering against the wall behind her. At first the girl had thought the man had sneezed or vomited and it grossed her out, but not half as much as when she realized what really had happened.

The customer who had spewed on her dropped to his knees and his body fell against the counter and then slid sideways to the tan tiled floor. He left a streak of blood and brain matter on the counter wall that looked like half a gruesome rainbow.

Audrey screamed, less from seeing the man collapse and more from the burning sensation she felt on the left side of her face as she realized she had been struck with something more than the man's blood as part of his face had been blown away. She fell to her knees clutching her face whose blood was now mixing with the dead man's. ER doctors would find bone fragments and two small pieces of the hollow point bullet that had been fired into the back of Detective Winter's head at point blank range.

The small sandwich shop didn't have any cameras but there had been two other customers sitting together at a small table when the shooting took place, a man and a woman. Neither of them actually heard a gunshot - she heard what she thought was a heavy drawer being slammed shut, he thought the sound was like a large wrench being dropped on pavement. Both had seen someone else in the shop but neither got a really good look at the individual - she thought it was a man at least six feet tall or more with a build like a football player and wearing a dark stocking cap, he said it was a black guy only about five-six who ran out of the store.

The boy working behind the register didn't see much but he was pretty sure the guy was tall, thin and from one of the terrorist countries and he was sure he heard him say, "Alla akbar" as he left. Two other eyewitnesses on the street made statements to the effect that the man coming out of the sandwich shop left on a motorcycle or in a black minivan. The homicide detectives on the scene had a lot of information that would lead them nowhere.

Marco wasn't sure exactly where he was other than in the parking lot of a twenty-four hour grocery store. His first hit on the three new targets had gone better than he could have hoped. He had gone to the detective's apartment and staked it out a block away with the expectation that he'd be waiting a number of hours for the man to get home. He was surprised when half an hour later he saw his target exit the building and walk to the sandwich shop.

Once Marco realized the shop didn't have security cameras, he put on a dark jacket, ball cap and gloves and walked calmly into the establishment, the silenced pistol at his side. He shot the cop in the back of the head and walked just as calmly out, walked a block away, cut through an alley and returned to his car. The old school mafia had perfected the art of assassination in broad daylight in front of dozens of witnesses, the more the better, because everyone saw or heard something different and gave conflicting accounts to the police. Eyewitness testimony was the worst sort of evidence and detectives hated it when that's all they had to go off of.

It felt good to drop the target so effortlessly, not because Marco liked to kill but because it meant he was that much closer - a third of the way - to rescuing his woman. But now as he contemplated his next target and next move he thought that if he wasn't careful he could be killing Ophelia. He needed to find out who it was that had her and what their connection was to the list of cops he was supposed to off.

Marco refused to let his mind consider the possibility that Ophelia was already dead. He had been given no proof of life and the number he'd originally called was no longer in service. He knew it was likely that all of his killing could be for naught, but he'd already set it in his mind that he'd kill every motherfucker on the planet if that's what it took to get his woman back. And if she was dead, then not even God himself could help those who were responsible.

The fact that they had gotten to Dmitri, killing him and his wife - he'd found the news stories online - concerned him greatly. Dmitri had obviously compromised this current mission, but it was nearly impossible these days to withstand the torture techniques and chemicals available to interrogators. All it usually came down to was how long you could hold out and the fact that Ophelia was nabbed less than sixteen hours later meant Dmitri hadn't held out long.

It was that very reason Marco kept his life very compartmentalized and nobody knowing more than one or two pieces of his world and how it operated. Unfortunately Dmitri did know about one of Marco's properties as well as his plane, which meant he would have to liquidate them. Marco never grew attached to material possessions and with his bankroll their loss would be little felt. He'd already ditched the Toyota Avalon after having found the tracking device and placing it on the undercarriage of another white Toyota found at a shopping mall. Once again Marco had kicked himself for not being on top of his game; he should have searched the car before ever leaving the airstrip. But he and Ophelia had been talking about their honeymoon plans to the Maldives and the glass floored bungalows that sat out over the water. He should have been concentrating more on his mission at hand, not talking to her; hell, he should have known better than to even have her along. He needed to pull it together and start doing this right.

Detective Ken Hansel separated from his wife sleeping in the bed beside him, having the feeling something was wrong. He pulled his .40 out of the holster on the nightstand that was in front of the digital clock that read 2:23. He had gotten home a little before midnight to find his worried wife Peggy waiting for him. Everyone in Sacramento who had a radio, television or computer knew about the police officer who had been killed execution style and the other detective whose death was originally considered an accident but was now upgraded to suspicious.

Hansel was sure footed moving quietly through the gray shadows of the upstairs bedroom and into the hallway. With the barrel of his Glock he scratched his crotch through his red bikini briefs that his wife had bought him. He stopped and peered into one of the doorways along the hallway; both his young daughters, six and eight were asleep in their comfy beds with their fluffy comforters. A little further down the hall he checked on his fourteen year old son who slept half in and half on a single sheet.

He continued downstairs where all was quiet, too quiet. He couldn't put his finger on it but what he could put his finger on was the trigger of his sidearm as he moved like a wraith through the black and gray shadows of his home. He reached the kitchen and saw their border collie, Buddy, lying in front of the refrigerator. That's what was missing, Hansel thought, the sound of Buddy's breathing and shuffling and nails clicking on the floor.

The detective didn't make a sound as he knelt down with his gun at the ready and with his free hand checked the dog. The body was warm and he didn't feel any blood but also didn't feel a heartbeat or any motions of breathing coming from the animal.

And then he felt the barrel of a gun pressed against the back of his head. Whoever it was had come up behind him without a sound, no brushing of fabric, no scuff of a shoe, no exhalation of breath. Hansel knew immediately the man was a professional and what that meant for the cop.

Hansel slowly raised his hands up, letting the Glock dangle upside down from the trigger guard around his finger. "Please," the detective said, his voice low, his mouth dry, "not in the house where my kids will find me."

"How do you know I'm not going to kill them, too?" the man said coldly behind him, his voice with a hint of foreign accent, though Hansel couldn't place where. The gun was snatched away from Hansel's finger.

"Because it's obvious you're a professional," the cop said. "The fact that you're here means you're taking down the whole crew."

"Who's in the crew?"

"You've already killed Sergeant and Winters. I knew that wasn't an accident at the gym as soon as I--"

"Who else is in this crew?" The unseen man pressed the barrel of his gun hard into the back of Hansel's head.

"Fox and Cole. Please, have a shred of decency and do me outside."

"Get up. Slowly." Hansel did so. "Tell me where to find them and I'll grant your request."

"You obviously know where to find us," Hansel said, "or you wouldn't be here." The barrel was still touching the back of Hansel's head and he considered this a good thing, especially seeing as the perpetrator was still wanting information.

At least twice a year for the past decade Hansel attended law enforcement seminars practicing disarming techniques, advanced self defense tactics, hostage and terrorist negotiation and psychology, and a myriad of other useful skills. He had disarmed at least a hundred attackers on the mat with practice knives and replica handguns pressed to his head, neck and back.

He took a breath and it was the last thing he ever did as the hitman pulled the trigger and his brains were blown across the kitchen. Hansel's body fell atop the strangled dog's body.

Marco had heard the intake of breath and saw the cop's shoulders begin to tense. He knew the cop had to try something and he was ready and waiting for it. Marco had been on his share of martial arts mats in his lifetime but the difference between him and just about everyone else holding a weapon to the back of someone's head was that Marco had already set in his mind they were dead, whereas anyone else in the same position was likely trying to rob the person or make them do something and only intended to hurt them as a last resort. For Marco it was priority number one, no fucking around.

"Fucking do it already," Detective Leonard Cole told the man holding the gun on him. Cole was lying in bed, the sky outside his bedroom window going from gray to blue as the sun made its way around the planet for another sunrise. Beside Cole, with two holes in her bloody chest, was Cole's dead girlfriend. She had awakened screaming at the sight of the man in their room and as the hitman put two bullets into her Cole reached for his handgun that was no longer next to his bed. Now he was pissed and just wanted it over with. "If you're going to do it, do it."

"Why would Fox want the whole crew eliminated?" the hitman asked Cole.

"I should have fucking known!" Cole said as he sat up in bed, his back against the cherry oak headboard. His feet were still under the covers so there was no way to kick at the assassin who was standing back further than arm's reach anyway. Cole kept looking for an opening without looking like he was looking. The coppery smell of blood was strong in the room, as was the smell of piss when his girlfriend's bowels let loose upon her demise.

"That doesn't answer my question," the killer said.

"Fox is a piece of shit. He's been stealing from our crew and ripping us off every chance he could."

"Where can I find him?"

"He has an apartment, but I'm pretty sure he's not there. We found him at the casino but he probably wouldn't be stupid enough to return there."

"You're telling me everywhere I can't find him." The hitman's gun with the silencer attachment raised level with Cole's forehead.

"I'm trying to help you!" Cole said frantically. "I want to see him dead. I'll pay you. Double, even triple. Whatever you want."

"What I want only Fox has."

Cole nodded his head vigorously. "I'll help you find him."

"All you've told me is where he isn't. Do you know where he is?"

"No, but we can work together. I'll tell you everything I know."

Marco listened and made a few notes and then put two bullets into Cole's chest. He didn't work well with others and he would never trust a cop.

# CHAPTER 22

"You know we can't trust that dirty cop," Charlie said. "I mean, I don't trust any cop but he's totally off the chain."

"Let's just do this," Evan said as he parked the Lexus at a small park across from a water treatment plant. The sun had risen on the drive from The Detective's stash house. He had wakened them less than a half hour prior and told them what they were going to do.

Evan and Charlie had fallen asleep together on the couch, having slipped their shoes off and then Charlie being spooned snuggled up against Evan. She could feel his hardness pushing against the back of her thigh and one of his forearms rested between her breasts. She didn't mind and was glad to be held by him.

Sometime in the middle of the night Charlie awoke to seeing The Detective looking at the living room TV with his back to her, his hand scratching his hairy butt cheek. A newscaster was talking about a city in panic as two more members of the sheriff's department had been found executed within the past eight hours.

Charlie closed her eyes before he turned around, pretending to be asleep. She could feel his molesting eyes on her for a long time before he finally went back to the bedroom.

She was glad to be out of that house and had no intention of ever returning. The Detective had told them this was the last thing they had to do, and whether or not Charlie and Evan believed him, they didn't have much choice.

The Detective had handed Evan a locked metal camera case and told them to bring it to a particular house.

"You mean like leave it on the doorstep?" Evan had asked.

"No. I want you to leave it inside, next to the furnace," the cop told him. "Don't worry, nobody's home." He had checked his computer and the GPS tracking software showed the car to be on the other side of town, though he had no idea the tracking device had been placed on a different vehicle.

The camera case weighed about ten pounds and Evan asked what was in it, though he had somewhat of an idea.

"You ask too many questions," The Detective told him. "Now get the fuck out of here and do what I told you."

On the drive across town Evan and Charlie contemplated opening the suitcase with their lock picks but decided against it thinking the thing could be booby-trapped.

"Oh shit," Evan said as they got out of the Lexus at the park.

Charlie's eyes darted to the camera case hanging at Evan's side. "What?"

"We forgot the suitcase with the loot from the last job."

"Go back and get it if you want, but not me."

Evan shook his head. "We can see what this place has since we'll be inside anyway."

"Let's just dump the case and get the hell out of here, far away."

"Come on, we take a few minutes to check the regular spots. It would be stupid not to."

"Whatever," Charlie said as they walked down the street with houses on only one side of it. A couple cars could be seen backing out of garages and driveways as commuters headed off to work.

When they reached their target house and Evan saw it was a two-story home, he said, "Maybe you're right, we should just drop off the case inside and go."

"No, you were right," Charlie countered, "makes no sense to break into a house and not at least see if there's anything worth taking."

The front entrance to the house was secluded by a small porch and a couple large bushes. And seeing as there were no homes across the street, only passing cars would be able to see them, but anyone up this early wouldn't be looking at anything but to get to work.

Charlie rang the doorbell.

"What are you doing? He said nobody was home," Evan said.

"Like I'm going to believe anything that comes out of his mouth."

She rang the doorbell again and then produced her lock picks and a minute later they were inside the house and locking the door behind them. "Set that down," she said to Evan, motioning to the camera case. "We'll put it where it belongs when we're done."

Evan set the case against the wall in the living room and then reluctantly followed Charlie up the stairs and to the master bedroom. In the bland room Charlie went to the dresser while Evan checked the nightstands.

"What the fuck," Charlie said as she pulled open each of the drawers to find them empty.

"There's nothing in the nightstands," Evan said, "and I mean nothing."

Charlie checked the master bathroom while Evan looked in the walk-in closet.

"No one lives here," Evan said. "It's like one of those houses staged for sale, you know--"

"Sh," Charlie said and grabbed his arm, her head cocked toward the bedroom door.

Evan heard it, too, someone opening the front door.

Sasha opened the door and screamed. It was the spare bedroom at Fox's stash house and she wasn't sure what had prompted her to even look in the room. Now that everyone had left the house, except her and Fox, or so she thought, she had walked naked to the kitchen hoping to find something to drink but only coming away with water. She was also getting hungry and didn't know of any restaurants that delivered food in the morning so she and Fox were going to have to go out somewhere. These were the thoughts running through her mind as she walked naked down the hallway and saw the closed door that she curiously opened.

Fox was sitting naked in bed with the laptop computer heating his thighs. He was checking the monitoring website to see where the tracking device was showing the car to be. It was still in the same spot it was the last time he'd checked hours ago, which he considered a little odd. He was hoping to find it in motion back to the house where he'd sent the burglars, or ideally already there because then he could make a single call and take care of all of his loose ends in one big bang.

He heard Sasha scream and in the same motion Fox was pushing the laptop off his legs and grabbing his handgun from the nightstand and running for the hallway. Oh shit, he thought as he saw Sasha standing in the doorway of the spare bedroom.

"Who the fuck is this?" Sasha screamed. "What's going on?"

"Stop sticking your nose where it doesn't belong!" Fox yelled as he yanked her out of the doorway and then pulled the spare bedroom door shut.

On the other side of the door lay Ophelia handcuffed in a twin bed with duct tape over her mouth. The dress she wore and the bedclothes beneath her stunk of her urine as she'd been confined to the bed for nearly eighteen hours. Her throat was dry and sore, she had hunger pangs and was dehydrated. She kept dozing in and out of consciousness and had been sleeping until she heard the scream and saw the naked woman in the doorway. Then just as quickly the naked man appeared and the door was slammed shut. Ophelia didn't have enough moisture in her body to cry.

"The lady's a suspect and a material witness," Fox told Sasha as he dragged her back to the bedroom.

"Then why isn't she at the sheriff's department?" Sasha asked.

"Because the cops are in on it. You saw what they did to us at the casino. You don't know everything that's going on, so you just need to trust me, okay?"

Sasha sniffled and nodded her head. "How much longer do you have to hold her?"

"It will all be wrapped up today and then we can go wherever you want."

Marco didn't want to return to the vacation rental but he didn't want to have his suitcases and especially some of his assassin's tools that he didn't need in the car while he was out doing hits. If he'd had to abandon the car he didn't want anything that he couldn't leave behind. Yet as soon as he walked into the house he knew someone was there, he could smell them. And then he could hear them whispering and shuffling around upstairs.

Marco pulled out his silenced handgun. He should have known they'd come for him or be waiting for him to return. He moved across the foyer to the stairs but then something caught his eye down the long hallway that led to the kitchen and a set of French doors that opened to the backyard. A pair of legs were dangling from the second floor.

Marco rushed silently down the hallway, through the kitchen and swung open the French doors just as a teenage girl dropped to the ground. He tackled her, looping an arm around her throat and putting the gun to her head.

"No!" a voice screamed from up above.

Marco shifted his weight and rolled so that he was on his back with the girl's body covering his as he pointed his gun at the figure in the second floor window.

The young man showed his bare hands and said, "Don't shoot! There's a bomb in the house."

Evan wasn't exactly sure why he said that. It just seemed that he needed to say something important to keep from being shot and to make the man not hurt Charlie. "Please, stop choking her," Evan begged.

Marco loosened his stranglehold slightly, enough for Charlie to cough for breath. But she tried to remain as still as possible so as not to provoke the man with the gun.

"Get down here!" Marco told the guy in the window.

"I... I can't. I'm afraid of heights."

"More than you're afraid of bullets?" Marco asked. "You have two seconds to make a decision."

"Ah, man," Evan said as he shakily climbed out of the window. "Oh god, I can't do this," he said as he slowly did it. He hung from the windowsill and looked down. "No, it's too far, I can't," he said as he began to pull himself back up.

Marco squeezed the trigger and the wooden window frame two inches from Evan's right hand exploded into splinters.

"Agh!" Evan cried as he let go of the window with his right hand and then his left hand slipped and he was falling backwards.

Marco rolled out of the way, pulling the girl with him as Evan crashed to the grass.

"Wow, that wasn't so bad," Evan said and then looked into the barrel of the gun pointing at his face.

It took Evan and Charlie almost forty minutes to explain everything of how they were mixed up with The Detective - Marco told them the detective's name was Bryce Fox - and how he'd forced them to bring the bomb to this house and they were supposed to call him once it was planted.

Marco listened and asked questions but all he really wanted to know was if they'd seen Ophelia.

"You sure she wasn't black?" Evan asked.

"No, I told you, she's Persian," Marco told him.

"Some Persians can be black," Evan stated. " I know a friend who had a Persian cat that--"

Marco bonked him on the top of his head with the barrel of his gun. "She's not black."

"Ow!" Evan said rubbing his head. "I already had a concussion."

"You're about to have another," Marco said.

"There was another bedroom in the house," Charlie said. "She could be--"

"Take me there."

Fox was almost there as he fucked Sasha. She was on her back and he was atop her between her legs. He had his hands gripped to her ankles which were almost touching her ears. All of her dancing made her quite flexible and there wasn't a position in her Kama Sutra book she couldn't pull off. But for now she wished he'd just get off, both figuratively and literally. She wanted to get out of this house and away from him and she didn't think she was going to come back. He could keep all of his false promises; they weren't worth the bullshit that came along with them.

"Are you gonna come or not?" Sasha asked as drops of sweat fell from his body to hers.

"I'm almost there," he panted. "Stick a finger in my ass."

"What?"

"Your finger," Fox said as his cock slammed in and out of her pussy, "shove it up my ass."

"That's gross! Shove your own finger up your ass."

Fox kept fucking and considered that for a moment but then disregarded it as being as effective as trying to tickle yourself.

"You can't come because you keep smoking that fucking crack," Sasha said. And it was one more reason she knew she wouldn't be returning. He knew how she felt about that shit. But Fox didn't care about anyone but himself, that had always been obvious. "Do you want to tittie fuck me?"

"I told you what I want," he grunted, his balls slapping her ass with his every thrust. "Either stick something in my ass or I'll stick something in yours."

Sasha's eyes got wide but she knew better than to try to argue with him. She turned her head and looked at the nightstand. His gun was there, but that wasn't what she wanted. She reached out her hand and grabbed the crack pipe and shoved it into his asshole.

"Oh yeah," he groaned and his hips jackhammered into her as he spewed forth his man juice.

Shortly thereafter she told him she needed to go home to get some things. She got dressed and he told her not to be long, that they'd be leaving state before sunset. She was already thinking she'd be leaving state before that, maybe go spend some time with her cousins in Reno.

As Sasha opened the front door, she was accosted by three people. "Fox, your niece and nephew are here!" she called out.

Fox stepped out of the hallway saying, "I told you guys to call not--" Then he saw Marco, who was raising up a pistol. Sasha screamed as Fox dove back down the hallway. He scrambled toward the bedroom and the gun under his bed as Marco pushed Sasha into the house and ran toward the hallway. Evan and Charlie were standing at the edge of the living room wondering what they were supposed to do. Evan eyed the green suitcase by the couch thinking that they'd at least be able to grab their loot.

The house exploded with the sound of an AK-47 fully automatic assault rifle being fired down the hallway. Everyone dove for cover as the living room TV exploded and sheetrock and wood chips flew in every direction. The gunfire ceased and a smoky haze drifted from out of the hallway. A door opened and slammed shut.

Marco pointed his gun down the hallway looking for movement. The woman who had answered the door got up and made a run for the front door. Marco grabbed her with an arm around her throat, her body in front of his. Evan and Charlie were crouched down for cover by the couch.

A door down the hallway opened and Fox appeared in the smoky haze. His arm was around Ophelia's throat and he was using her as a shield. Her hands were cuffed in front of her and she had duct tape over her mouth but all that Marco cared about was that she was alive. Fox held a large hunting knife in the hand attached to the arm across Ophelia's throat. In his other hand Fox held his service sidearm.

Both men were pointing their guns at the other, each with the other's woman as a shield and hostage. Just as Marco was about to say something about a Mexican standoff, Fox fired his gun, the bullet exploding through Sasha's left tit and into her heart, killing her instantly. Marco dove for cover behind the loveseat. Fox knew he'd have to kill Sasha eventually, she knew too much.

"Throw out your gun or your woman dies," Fox said. "This is your only chance."

Marco threw his gun out toward the hallway.

"And your backup piece."

"Then she dies."

"No, she dies if you don't do exactly as I say."

Marco pulled a compact 9mm from his waistband and tossed it out.

"Now stand up."

"Let her go."

"I'm not going to tell you again."

Marco slowly stood up from behind the loveseat.

"Mmph!" Ophelia screamed behind the duct tape as Fox brought his gun up to bear on Marco. Ophelia hit Fox's arm as Marco dove to the floor. The bullet thudded into the wall.

"Here!" Evan yelled to Marco, throwing him the revolver from the green suitcase.

Fox was rushing toward the living room when Marco rolled onto his side and shot at the dirty cop from the bottom edge of the loveseat. Fox got off one shot that hit the top of the loveseat and then he was thrown off his feet as four .44 slugs pummeled his body.

Marco was up on his feet as Fox crumpled to the floor a lifeless bloody pile of flesh. Marco jumped over him to where Ophelia lay on the hallway floor. He crouched down and took her in his arms. Her head lolled to the side, her throat having been slit all the way to the spinal cord. Marco set her gently back to the floor and then walked out of the hallway and out of the house.

Evan stood and helped Charlie up, their ears ringing from all of the gunfire, their nostrils taking in all the white smoke. They stared at each other, neither wanting to look at the dead bodies.

Marco returned to the living room carrying the camera case. He'd examined it before they left the vacation rental determining there was enough plastic explosives to take out a city block. He had disarmed the cell phone trigger and now as he opened the case he set a timer.

"There are safes in the basement," Evan said. "A lot of them."

"Unless you can open and empty them in less than a minute, I suggest you get out." With that Marco walked out of the house. Evan and Charlie ran after him and piled into his car.

A quarter of a mile away Evan and Charlie looked out the back window at the huge explosion.

# CHAPTER 23

The sky was filled with orange, yellow and red for as far as the eye could see, the sunset exploding across the California skyline. Evan and Charlie were standing atop a desert hill in the middle of nowhere as they watched the big ball of flame slowly melt into the horizon.

They had been driving in Charlie's GMC Envoy with her at the wheel for more than five hours. She preferred back roads over main thoroughfares and seeing as they had no specific destination in mind, no road was the wrong road. Evan only knew they were still in California because at the last intersection there was a sign pointing south that read: Death Valley 86 Miles. They had continued going east until Charlie turned onto a bumpy dirt road that led to the spot where they currently were.

"Our last California sunset," Charlie said as she stood in front of the SUV, her hand leaning on the hood. She was wearing a pair of dark blue, purple and pink yoga pants and a sleeveless blue and black sweatshirt with a zipper that was open enough to show glimpses of her pink bra every now and then depending on how she moved.

Evan stood beside her in a pair of jeans and a white and green checkerboard shirt. He was looking at the sunset and then looking at her when she spoke again. "I like to watch the sunset any time I leave a state, kind of like the closing chapter of a book."

"Have you seen a lot of sunsets?" Evan asked.

"More than I can count on one hand."

"You know, now that The Detective is dead, we don't really have to run."

"I don't like to stay in one place too long," Charlie said. "I'm a little surprised you wanted to come."

"It's been awhile since I've been on a road trip. I mean, you did want me to come, right?"

"Five hours on the road and now you're asking if I want you along?" She smiled and said, "I'm kidding, of course I want you to come."

"Really?"

"Really what?"

"You want me to come?"

"O-M-G, you are such a perv," Charlie said and went to shove his shoulder but he was already turning towards her and her momentum caused her to fall into him.

Evan threw out his hands to catch her, one of them landing on her left breast and the other on her hip as her body pressed against his.

"Oops, sorry," Evan said as he pulled his hand away from her boob. Charlie reached for his hand and put it back on her boob. She kept her body pressed into him as she looked into his eyes.

"That doesn't feel like a sprayer in your pocket," she said.

"Oh, it sprays alright."

"You're the biggest pervert I know."

"And I think you like it."

Charlie smiled at him and nodded. "I never said being a pervert was bad thing."

Evan squeezed her boob gently as he tilted his head down and slowly brought his mouth to hers. Her lips were warm and soft and full and tasted like the Juicy Fruit gum she'd been chewing. Charlie's hands went around his waist and she squeezed his body tightly against hers.

Charlie's pink tongue slipped between her lips and poked into Evan's mouth. She felt something of his poking harder into her midsection, straining against his jeans. Their kiss grew more passionate, both of their tongues now dancing in each other's mouths. Evan continued squeezing her tit with one hand while his other hand slid behind her and rubbed her ass.

Charlie moaned pleasantly in his mouth as she slipped one of her hands in between them and pulled the zipper of her sweatshirt down. She wiggled out of the garment and threw it onto the hood of her truck. Evan's hand cupped her breast through the pink bra, his thumb feeling the hardened nipple beneath.

Evan pushed her back against the grille of the Envoy, his aching crotch grinding against her as they kept their mouths glued together in a perpetual kiss. Evan's hand pushed the fabric of her bra cup aside and he took her tit in his hand, her stiff nipple tickling his palm. His other hand slipped behind her neck and his fingers pushed through her hair as he kissed her with every ounce of his being.

Charlie wanted more of him, all of him, and her hands tugged at his jeans. She got the button undone and then pulled on the zipper but it didn't move. The kissing continued as did the squeezing of her breast and pinching of her nipple as Charlie brought both her hands to Evan's crotch and yanked on the zipper.

She pulled away from his kiss and looked down between them in frustration. "I didn't know I was going to need my lock picks to get into your pants," she said.

"Huh-uh," Evan said as he brought his hands to his jeans and tore them open, busting the zipper. "This is straight up breaking and entering."

"Well then enter me already," Charlie said as she spun around and leaned over the hood of the SUV. She looped her thumbs over the waistband of her yoga pants and underwear and pulled them over the hump of her ass and down to her knees.

Evan's mouth watered and the tip of his dick dripped at the sight of her smooth white ass and her bare pink pussy peeking out below. His jeans fell to his knees and he tore the waistband of his boxers yanking them over his rock hard cock. He took his cock in hand and leaned forward, his other hand squeezing and parting Charlie's ass cheek. Her elbows and tits, one still uncovered, felt the heat of the truck's engine as they rested on the hood of the SUV. She looked over her shoulder anxiously at Evan whose eyes were glued to her ass.

Charlie sucked in her breath as she felt the thick head of Evan's prick graze her pussy lips and then felt herself being opened by him. Evan's knees were bent to give him the right height as he slid his throbbing cock into her warm, moist pinkness. He watched as his rod sank into her, both his hands on her ass cheeks and spreading them to give him a better view of his handiwork.

Charlie liked how he was pulling her ass cheeks apart while at the same time filling her pussy with his thickness. She moaned loudly into the desert as he pushed deeper into her - she wasn't sure if she could take any more of him - then she felt his pelvis grinding against her ass.

"Oh god," Evan groaned, his cock completely sheathed in her warmth. He clutched her ass, gritted his teeth and squeezed his keigel muscles to keep from coming right then and there she felt so damn good. He didn't want to embarrass himself by coming as soon as he stuck it in her or she might not give him another chance.

"Quit being a tease, you perv," Charlie said over her shoulder. "You made it inside, now find the goods."

Evan smiled thinking it was all good. He looked at her as he pulled his hips back, his cock feeling the arid desert air as it came out of her, and then he pushed back into her.

"Oh yes," she said as she turned away and threw her head back. He thrust into her again and felt her moving her hips to meet him. He grabbed her hair as he thrust into her again, pulling her head back.

"No, I don't like that," Charlie said.

Evan let go and brought his hands to her bra strap as he continued fucking her. He got the bra off and grasped both her titties in his hands, pinching her nipples between his fingers.

"Yes, I like that," she moaned.

Evan kept pounding her from behind.

"And that," she replied.

Evan's hips went wild with a flurry of motion and he gripped Charlie's tits like handholds as he spurted his fluids into her. He kept thrusting into her, slower now, until his legs began to quiver from exertion. He draped his body over the top her hers bent over the hood.

They both lay there looking westward. The sun had disappeared and the shades of red were transforming to deep blues and purples.

"You didn't come," Evan said.

"Not this time. But there will be more chances, right?"

"It's a good thing you're with a pervert."

Charlie squeezed her keigel muscles, in turn giving Evan's cock a squeeze, as a plane buzzed the sky overhead.

Marco kept the plane flying southeast at an altitude of 11,500 feet as he flew over the desert landscape. He kept a close eye on the LCD screens in the cockpit because there were a number of military no-fly zones he had to be sure to avoid. Of course it would be a quick way to end everything, simply fly towards Area 51 or a dozen other government installations and ignore all radio chatter until his small plane was blown out of the sky.

But Marco had never been suicidal - he'd always been a fighter. And though he felt numb right now, he was certain the pain of his loss would come and when it did he'd find a way to kill it like he did everything in his life.

He'd been a fool to let any semblance of true love enter his world. It had snuck up on him like a thief crawling into his window in the middle of the night, intruding into his dreams and filling his head with every fanciful thought that he knew he could never truly have. And now, because of him, the most beautiful woman he'd ever known was dead.

Behind the plane, the sunset slowly dissipated as Marco flew deeper into the darkness.

## About the Author

D. Mann has spent more than half his adult life in state and federal prisons due to less than optimal decisions. You may contact the author through Deviant Ways Publications.

---

Follow Deviant Ways Publications for information and updates on more exciting reads at:

www.DeviantWaysPublications.com

www.Facebook.com/Deviant.Ways.Publications/

Deviant Ways Publications
PO Box 94
Montrose, MN 55363

*Also available through Deviant Ways Publications!*

**The Money Shot**

Duncan just came into a whole bunch of cash.
Unfortunately, the folks who printed it want it back!
Midlife crisis with a backpack full of money, what's one to do? ROAD TRIP! Chasing the dream while being chased has never been more fun - unless you get caught by the people chasing you! Then there's the strippers, the feds... Everyone wanting to take:

*The Money Shot*

# IN ME I TRUST
## An Adult Choose Your Own Adventure

It's another day in the life of a hustler and you've got decisions to make. Are you going to hit the streets and get on your grind or will you screw around and trick it off? You'll need to think fast and do the right thing - which doesn't necessarily mean the legal thing - if you're going to make it to the top and stay out of the hospital, prison, and the morgue.

With forty-six separate endings and hundreds of different paths to take to reach your destiny, no day will ever be the same. Bank robberies, drug deals, kidnapping, gun running, burglary, murder for hire, and more can lead to success or failure, it's your choice. With pages full of sex, drugs, violence, federal agents, car chases, shootouts, double crosses and backstabbing, you know that the struggle is real and sometimes it feels good to be a gangster.

www.ingramcontent.com/pod-product-compliance
Lightning Source LLC
Chambersburg PA
CBHW051944290426
44110CB00015B/2104